LAST DAY STRATEGIES FOR
RECAPTURING OUR FAMILIES,
OUR CITIES AND OUR NATION

the
joshua
generation
GOD'S CONQUERING MANIFESTO

dr. michael maiden

The Joshua Generation: God's Conquering Manifesto
Copyright 2005
by Dr. Michael Maiden
ISBN 0-9720650-2-4

Published by
Joshua Generation Publishing
11640 N 19th Ave
Phoenix, AZ 85029

CONTENTS

PREFACE

"Moses is dead." The cry quickly filled all the tents of the camp of the children of Israel. Their beloved leader had died. God's chosen vessel was gone. What would now happen to the great nation that God had delivered from bondage through the hands of Moses? Who could now lead God's people? What would God's next step be in to bring His children into their promised land?

God was ready. Ready to unveil a "new breed" of leader who was to lead the "new breed" of Israelite. God had been preparing a champion who would lead a nation of champions. His name was Joshua. He was the leader of the Joshua Generation.

For 40 years the Joshua Generation watched as their parents died off, one by one, on the wrong side of Jordan. Although God had supernaturally delivered and preserved them, they chaffed at this command to cross the River Jordan and possess the Promised Land. They were in a passive position of living in fear and unbelief. They were satisfied with just being delivered from Egypt. Yet God had not delivered His children from Egypt to let them die in the wilderness. His saving them from slavery was to be the first step in bringing them into their inheritance: a land of milk and honey - the Promised Land.

TYPES AND SHADOWS: OUR EXAMPLES

In 1 Corinthians 10:11 we read, "Now all these things happened to them as examples, and they were written for our admonition, upon whom the ends of the ages have come."

The Scriptures record the history and detail of the children of Israel for one purpose: for our learning, encouragement and example. In Romans 15:4 there can be found another confirmation of God's purpose for giving us the Old Testament: "For whatever things were written before were written for our learning, that we through the patience and comfort of the Scriptures might have hope."

God has given us both the unveiled, revealed doctrine and teaching of the New Testament and the veiled, hidden types and shadows of the Old Testament. As Christians, we receive our doctrine and foundational beliefs from the teaching of the New Testament. Then, through the eyes of the New, we look with new understanding and depth at the Old. For God has given us, in the Old Testament, a beautiful marriage of example to flow with New Testament teaching. As many have said before:

The Old Testament is in the New explained.
The New Testament is in the Old contained.

The Old Testament is in the New revealed.
The New Testament is in the Old concealed.

The Old Testament is in the New unfolded.
The New Testament is in the Old enfolded.

With this understanding, then let us look at the children of Israel and their journey into the Promised Land.

Moses is a type of the Lord Jesus Christ in that he was a deliverer to an entire nation. Like Christ at His birth, Satan sought to kill Moses by destroying all male children. However, Moses, like Jesus, was supernaturally saved. Moses was the meekest man on the earth (Numbers 12:3) as was Christ. Moses was called to go before Pharaoh and command him to let God's people go. Pharaoh means "the spoiler king." Pharaoh is a type of Satan, the arch enemy of God and man. The children of Israel were in Egypt, which literally means "place of double-limiting extremes." Egypt is a perfect type of

the world. Jesus has come to deliver us from the authority of
Satan (Pharaoh) and the power of the world (Egypt).

God's ultimate instrument in delivering His people from
Pharaoh and Egypt was in the Passover. God sent His angel of
death to kill the first-born of every living thing, except where
the blood of a spotless lamb was found over the doorpost.
That blemish-free lamb was a beautiful picture of the Blood
of Christ. John the Baptist called out as Jesus came to him to
be baptized in water, "The next day John saw Jesus coming
toward him, and said, "Behold! The Lamb of God who takes
away the sin of the world!" (John 1:29.)

Revelation 5:9 tells us about the Blood of Jesus: "And they
sang a new song, saying: 'You are worthy to take the scroll,
and to open its seals; for You were slain, and have redeemed
us to God by Your blood out of every tribe and tongue and
people and nation'...." In Colossians 1:14 we read, "in whom
we have redemption through His blood, the forgiveness of
sins."

By the Blood of Jesus, Satan's power over us has been broken, and we are delivered from the control of the world.

After the children of Israel were released from Egypt, they
were suddenly being chased again by the armies of Pharaoh
and Egypt. God opened up the waters of the Red Sea, and
they passed over to the other side. As the armies of Egypt
chased them, the waters closed up and destroyed the armies

of Pharaoh. This great deliverance is a type of water baptism and its severing of the hold that Satan and the world has on us. Through water baptism, we break the power of Satan, the world and our flesh to control us, and we are freed to live for God.

After the victory at the Red Sea, God began to lead this vast nation by giving them a cloud by day (for protection from the desert sun) and a fire by night (for protection from the cold, from wild animals and from snakes). This cloud and fire is a picture of the baptism of the Holy Spirit and living everyday under the guidance and power of the Holy Spirit. For food, God gave the children of Israel manna from heaven. This bread of life is a type of the Word of God. Jesus said that man could not live by bread alone, but by every Word of God. (Matthew 4:4.)

Joshua, whose name means "savior," is also a type of Christ. The children of Israel are a type of Church - the Body of Christ. In Acts 7:38 it speaks of them as "the congregation in the wilderness with the Angel who spoke to him on Mount Sinai, and with our fathers, the one who received the living oracles to give to us."

The children of Israel were called the "church in the wilderness." So from these types, we can learn and gain wisdom as the Holy Spirit gives us understanding and revelation.

We live in the most exciting time in the history of the human race. Every day, history is being made all around us as time is rushing towards its final moments. World events of staggering significance are happening at a breathtaking pace, as God prepares to send Jesus back from heaven.

For the Christian, your place in this great final climax is tremendously important. For God has chosen you to be alive and a part of His great army in the final hour of world history. He has predestined you to be a part of the last day, overcoming, victorious church of Jesus Christ! He has saved His best for last, and you are His best! The Bible speaks of a great move of God in the last days that will exceed anything God has ever done before. We are standing on the edge of this great tidal wave of glory. We are the Joshua Generation!

CHAPTER 1:
POSSESSING THE LAND

Moses sent out twelve spies to spy out the promised land. God had already given them a command to go over Jordan into the promised land, as well as the assurance of His power and provision to protect them as they went. They camped and became comfortable just a few short miles from their land of promise.

Comfortable Christianity is powerless Christianity. God has not delivered and saved us from the world and the power of the enemy just to have us "make camp" on the wrong side of the river. It is true that the first thing God's power and love can do for us is to save us by the Blood of Christ, but God didn't save you to have you sit in a passive place of inactive Christianity. God saved you to make you a soldier in His great end-time army! True Christian living is found in an of-fensive, not defensive, position and purpose.

God told the children of Israel to possess the land. "See, I have set the land before you; go in and possess the land which the LORD swore to your fathers -- to Abraham, Isaac, and Jacob -- to give to them and their descendants after them." (Deuteronomy 1:8) "Look, the LORD your God has set the land before you; go up and possess it, as the LORD God of your fathers has spoken to you; do not fear or be discouraged." (Deuteronomy 1:21.) "Rise, take your journey, and cross over the River Arnon. Look, I have given into your hand Sihon the Amorite, king of Heshbon, and his land. Begin to possess it, and engage him in battle." (Deuteronomy 2:24.)

In fact, over forty times in the book of Deuteronomy alone, God commands the children of Israel to "possess the land." The Hebrew word "possess" means "to occupy by driving out the previous tenants and possessing in their place; to seize; to expel; to drive out; to ruin." It was a military word that gave an understanding of battling to possess, fighting to recover.

Believer, it is time for war! God is ready to invade families, cities and nations with His glory and grace, but He needs a believing church that will "possess" the land. It's time for you to possess your inheritance as a child of God. God has given you, literally, thousands of precious promises that make up your "promised land." God's Word is God's will for you and God's will for you is to be healed, blessed, prosperous and living in absolute victory! Everything God's Word declares, God wills for you to possess. But it takes an aggressive, faith-filled, possessing attitude, or else you will never "cross over" into God's best for you.

JOSHUA GENERATION OF LEADERS

The spies went and searched out the land for forty days and then came back to give their report. Ten of the spies reported that there were good, wonderful things and places over the river, but that there were also enemies there. They proceeded to describe the strength and stature (giants) of their enemies.

This speaks today of the negative, unbelieving teaching and preaching of ministers and religious leaders. Like the twelve spies, ministers and Christian leaders are called and anointed of God to bring His people into His inheritance for them. And like so many ministers today, the ten spies concluded that the promised land was nice, but there were giants there. How it grieves the heart of God when His leaders discourage instead of encourage the people of God! God's people are limited by the faith and vision of their leaders. That's why God is raising up a new breed of leader - leaders that dare to believe God for all He's promised to do. Leaders will be judged by the love, maturity and victory in which the people they've led live.

In these last days, God is raising up a Joshua Generation of believers: saints that don't retreat from the spiritual battle field, but courageously move on with God into His glory. Two spies did come back with a good report. As the people began to be flooded with fear and hopelessness by the report of the ten spies, Caleb lifted up his voice "and said, 'Let us go up at once and take possession, for we are well able to overcome it.' But the men who had gone up with him said, 'We are not able to go up against the people, for they are stronger than we.'" (Numbers 13:30, 31.)

Caleb had a "possessing" attitude. Caleb, whose name means "wholehearted, bold forcible attack," was a type of the Joshua Generation leader who exhorted and encouraged God's people to possess God's best.

God has not called you to just survive; He's called you to thrive! And the kingdom of God was not designed for passive, stationary, defeatist living. In Matthew 16:18,1 9 Jesus said this about the kingdom: "And I also say to you that you are Peter, and on this rock I will build My church, and the gates of Hades shall not prevail against it. And I will give you the keys of the kingdom of heaven, and whatever you bind on earth will be bound in heaven, and whatever you loose on earth will be loosed in heaven."

Jesus said the gates of hell can't stop the offensive attack of the Church. As long as you are living in a defensive or passive Christian attitude, you will not be able to partake of what God has for you.

The children of Israel did not listen to Caleb. Instead, they listened to the voice of the "negative ministers" who, by their evil report, robbed an entire generation of God's blessings. Religion will rob you from God's best if you let it. It was religious people who crucified Christ, and they are still doing it today by inflicting the doctrine of men upon deceived people. Caleb had a different spirit; he followed God fully. (Numbers 14:24.) God is raising up a generation of saints who have a different spirit than defeated, unbelieving, religiously ruined people. And, like Caleb, we will be brought "into the land" and our "seed shall possess it." (Numbers 14:24.)

The reason why God is birthing the spirit of victory and the spirit of war in His Church is simply this: whatever we don't conquer will conquer us. The reason that a passive Church has been so destructive in our land is that, because of our compromise, Satan's strongholds have gotten stronger and stronger, even to the point of invading the Body of Christ.

In Numbers 33:51-56 we read: "Speak to the children of Israel, and say to them: 'When you have crossed the Jordan into the land of Canaan, then you shall drive out all the inhabitants of the land from before you, destroy all their engraved stones, destroy all their molded images, and demolish all their high places; you shall dispossess the inhabitants of the land and dwell in it, for I have given you the land to possess.

"And you shall divide the land by lot as an inheritance among your families; to the larger you shall give a larger inheritance, and to the smaller you shall give a smaller inheritance; there everyone's inheritance shall be whatever falls to him by lot. You shall inherit according to the tribes of your fathers. But if you do not drive out the inhabitants of the land from before you, then it shall be that those whom you let remain shall be irritants in your eyes and thorns in your sides, and they shall harass you in the land where you dwell. Moreover it shall be that I will do to you as I thought to do to them.'"

God told them they couldn't ignore their enemies. They couldn't compromise with them in any way. These enemies are not flesh and blood to us, but they are Satan's strongholds and strategies that we are to recognize and war against as the Church.

Our lifestyle is not to be one of trying to survive Satan's attacks and worldly temptation. Our lifestyle is to be one of being on the attack, taking back what Satan has stolen from man.

In Ephesians 6:10-18 God lays out His battle plan for us: "Finally, my brethren, be strong in the Lord and in the power of His might. Put on the whole armor of God, that you may be able to stand against the Wiles of the devil. For we do not wrestle against flesh and blood, but against principalities, against powers, against the rulers of the darkness of this age, against spiritual hosts of wickedness in the heavenly places.

Therefore take up the whole armor of God, that you may be able to withstand in the evil day, and having done all, to stand.

"Stand therefore, having girded your waist with truth, having put on the breastplate of righteousness, and having shod your feet with the preparation of the gospel of peace; above all, taking the shield of faith with which you will be able to quench all the fiery Darts of the wicked one. And take the helmet of salvation, and the sword of the Spirit, which is the word of God; praying always with all prayer and supplication in the Spirit, being watchful to this end with all perseverance and supplication for all the saints...."

This scripture tells us that we are commanded to "be strong." Why? Because only those who have been made strong are fit for battle. And we are in a battle, like it or not. You are a part of God's army and He doesn't have any "conscientious objectors." Don't let any person, or even any preacher, tell you that we are not in a spiritual war. If you listen to that, you will become a casualty or a prisoner of war.

One spring picnic during my senior year in high school, the two biggest football players were picked for a game. Both of them were blindfolded and given pillows. Then they were told them to have a blindfolded pillow fight against each other. However, just before they started, the blindfold was taken off of one of the boys. Then they were told to start.

Well, the boy who took off his blindfold proceeded to pound the other mercilessly, until, in utter frustration, the other boy took off his blindfold and realized the joke was on him. Dear saints, don't let the joke be on you because you were taught that there is no battle. There is a war, and you need to prepare for it.

2 Corinthians 10:3-5 tells us that "though we walk in the flesh, we do not war according to the flesh. For the weapons of our warfare are not carnal but mighty in God for pulling down strongholds, casting down arguments and every high thing that exalts itself against the knowledge of God, bringing every thought into captivity to the obedience of Christ."

Here we see that not only are we in a war, but God has given us His own weapons to win. We are always called to win! Jesus described this war-like, overcoming attitude when He said, "And from the days of John the Baptist until now the kingdom of heaven suffers violence, and the violent take it by force." (Matthew 11:12) The NIV Bible reads: "...the kingdom of God has been forcefully advancing and forceful men lay hold of it."

God wants you to lay hold of the kingdom of God for your life and family and city. As a Christian, God's called you to the lifestyle of a warrior and a champion. God doesn't look for strong, courageous people -- He makes the weak and fearful strong, bold and courageous! Then He uses them. God's strength is your strength. God's courage is your courage. God's power is for you in this hour of destiny. Rise up and POSSESS THE LAND!

20 \\ THE JOSHUA GENERATION

CHAPTER 2:
PEOPLE OF VISION

The first thing the Lord did for Joshua after the death of
Moses was to give Joshua a clear-cut vision of the land He had
for Joshua and the Israelites. In Joshua 1:2-4, we read, "Moses
My servant is dead. Now therefore, arise, go over this Jordan,
you and all this people, to the land which I am giving to them
-- the children of Israel. Every place that the sole of your foot
will tread upon I have given you, as I said to Moses. From the
wilderness and this Lebanon as far as the great river, the River
Euphrates, all the land of the Hittites, and to the Great Sea
toward the going down of the sun, shall be your territory."

Every place he walked, every place he could see, God would
give him for their land. The Lord was building a vision of
possessing, a vision of victory, a vision of destiny into Joshua.
This vision of the promised land had begun many years earlier
when God spoke to a man named Abram. "And the LORD

said to Abram, after Lot had separated from him: "Lift your eyes now and look from the place where you are -- northward, southward, eastward, and westward; for all the land which you see I give to you and your descendants forever. And I will make your descendants as the dust of the earth; so that if a man could number the dust of the earth, then your descendants also could be numbered. Arise, walk in the land through its length and its width, for I give it to you." (Genesis 13:14-17)

God said to Abram, "Lift up now your eyes." God wants you to lift up your eyes, saint. He wants you to see His ability, His might, His precious promises, His endless love and grace. Your vision determines the course of your entire life. How God longs for us to see life the way He sees life. God literally spoke to Abram and said, "Whatever you can see, you can possess. If you can see it, you can have it." The very purpose of words and language is to form images that communicate. God's Word communicates God's vision and desire to the human race. God's Word is designed to bring vision to God's people. You are to see God's promises as yours. Until you see yourself receiving what God's Word has provided, it will not work for you.

Jesus said, in Matthew 6:22-23, "The lamp of the body is the eye. If therefore your eye is good, your whole body will be full of light. But if your eye is bad, your whole body will be full of darkness. If therefore the light that is in you is darkness, how great is that darkness!"

Jesus was not speaking about physical eyesight. He was speaking about spiritual eyesight. He was teaching about money. There is nothing evil about money unless your vision concerning it is evil. Jesus was not talking about what you see, but how you see. God wants to change the way you look at life. He wants to give you a vision for victory. He wants to build your faith-sight until life is not a burden but an adventure with Him.

When the twelve spies went over Jordan to spy out the land, they all saw the same physical things. But the way they saw is what separated the ten fearful and unbelieving spies from the two faith-filled ones. "Then Caleb quieted the people before Moses, and said, 'Let us go up at once and take possession, for we are well able to overcome it.' But the men who had gone up with him said, "We are not able to go up against the people, for they are stronger than we." And they gave the children of Israel a bad report of the land which they had spied out, saying, "The land through which we have gone as spies is a land that devours its inhabitants, and all the people whom we saw in it are men of great stature. There we saw the giants (the descendants of Anak came from the giants); and we were like grasshoppers in our own sight, and so we were in their sight."' (Numbers 13:30-33)

Verse 33 tells us, "and we were like grasshoppers in our own sight." The ten spies had grasshopper vision. They had not allowed all the tremendous miracles and deliverances that God had given them to build their faith and change their vision. Grasshopper vision always has an excuse why we can't do what God said we could do. I pastor an exploding, exciting church in Phoenix, Arizona. One of the reasons that we started a church in our town was because we were told that it was "tough soil" and a "hard area to break through." Well, God has broken through because we refused to receive grasshopper vision. At the very beginning of our church, I could tell the people, "I see thousands being saved and delivered and healed here." God has brought that vision to pass.

The prophet Elisha's vision was that God was in control and able to do what He said He would do. However, he had a problem with one of his "church staff." We read in 2 Kings 6:14-17 that the enemy had sent "horses and chariots and a great army there and they...surrounded the city" in which Elisha was living. The next morning "when the servant of the man of God arose early and went out, there was an army, surrounding the city with horses and chariots. And his servant said to him, 'Alas, my master! What shall we do?' So he answered, 'Do not fear, for those who are with us are more than those who are with them.' And Elisha prayed, and said, 'LORD, I pray, open his eyes that he may see.' Then the

LORD opened the eyes of the young man, and he saw. And behold, the mountain was full of horses and chariots of fire all around Elisha."

One morning Elisha's servant woke up to find a host of their enemy's armies surrounding their city. He ran to Elisha and cried, "Now what are we going to do?" His vision was limited to what his physical eyes could see. The current circumstance had filled his heart with fear and failure and hopelessness. Elisha prayed to God and asked God to open his servant's spiritual eyes. God did open the eyes of the servant and then everything changed. If the circumstances of your life have filled you with fear and failure, then pray and ask God to change your vision.

The Holy Spirit's prayer through the Apostle Paul in Ephesians 1:17-19 gives us a key in this area: "The God of our Lord Jesus Christ, the Father of glory, may give to you the spirit of wisdom and revelation in the knowledge of Him, the eyes of your understanding being enlightened; that you may know what is the hope of His calling, what are the riches of the glory of His inheritance in the saints, and what is the exceeding greatness of His power toward us who believe, according to the working of His mighty power."

The Holy Spirit will open the "eyes of your understanding" so you can know, from God's Word:

Who we are in Christ,
What we have in Christ
and What we can do in Christ

A godly vision destroys the limitations that the world, the flesh and the devil have used to hold you down. An ungodly vision keeps you in a circle of failure and fear. Proverbs 29:18 tells us, "Where there is no revelation, the people perish; but happy is he who keeps the law."

We find that in the New Covenant, the Holy Spirit leads and guides the Church through visions, dreams and prophecy. Acts 2:16-18 says, "But this is what was spoken by the prophet Joel: 'And it shall come to pass in the last days, says God, That I will pour out of My Spirit on all flesh; Your sons and your daughters shall prophesy, Your young men shall see visions, Your old men shall dream dreams. And on My menservants and on My maidservants I will pour out My Spirit in those days; And they shall prophesy.'"

Through revelation, God guides the Church. We are to be people flooded with Godly visions, dreams and prophecy. That is how God speaks and leads us in this hour.

Godly vision is so essential that if you don't change your vision from fear to faith, from failure to victory, God is limited and cut off by your unbelieving sight and He won't do much for you. This is not because He doesn't love you, but because He only responds to faith. If you take a person with an inward vision of failure and give them one million dollars in cash, it is painfully true that they will very likely lose all the money. This is because eventually, that vision of failure will produce in their physical circumstances. Fear is the result of a vision of failure. Fear is the enemy of God and all mankind. However, if you take that same man and woman and change his or her vision from fear to faith, and from failure to victory, and if you take everything they own away from them, then eventually they will get it all back and more. The inward vision of victory and success will eventually produce an outward manifestation of it.

In Habakkuk 2:2-3 the Word of God tells us to "write the vision and make it plain on tablets, that he may run who reads it. For the vision is yet for an appointed time; but at the end it will speak, and it will not lie. Though it tarries, wait for it; because it will surely come, it will not tarry."

Here the Lord tells us to write the vision. Write it so others can read it and run. Several years ago God spoke to me and said, "This day I give you the city." After the Lord spoke that to me, I shared it with our congregation of about ninety people. We then made a large banner and put it up on a wall in our sanctuary. We have prayed and proclaimed that vision, and now it is coming to pass. Vision is like a seed. If you plant it in your heart and water it with the Word of God in agreement, it will come to pass. Though it takes time, it will come to pass if you will not quit.

In 2 Corinthians 3:17-18 God's Word tells us that "the Lord is the Spirit; and where the Spirit of the Lord is, there is liberty. But we all, with unveiled face, beholding as in a mirror the glory of the Lord, are being transformed into the same image from glory to glory, just as by the Spirit of the Lord."

This scripture tells us that the image you see is the reality you will be. God's Word will transform you into the image of Christ as you receive and believe the precious promises it offers you. Remember:

Whatever you can see you can be!
Whatever you can see you can acheive!
Whatever you can see you can believe!

The first step to your possessing your promised land is for you to allow the Holy Spirit to birth in you Godly vision. That vision then becomes the blueprint of God's design in your life.

The Joshua Generation is a generation of people with world-changing vision.

The Joshua Generation is a generation of believers who believe nothing is impossible to God.

The Joshua Generation is an army that truly believes it cannot be defeated, and that believes the greatest move of God ever is now beginning in the earth.

CHAPTER 3:
PEOPLE OF PRAYER

The Lord spoke four times in the first chapter of Joshua and said, "Be strong and of a good courage." (Joshua 1:6, 7, 9, 18.) Four times God commands Joshua to "be strong." Why would God repeat this command verbatim to Joshua?

First of all, in spiritual warfare, "we must be strong to win." In the arena of spiritual battle, the strongest always wins. That's why God has offered to clothe us in His power and strength. We receive His power and strength in the place of prayer. Prayer is the source of strength, power and courage for the believer.

Ephesians 6:10-12 says, "Finally, my brethren, be strong in the Lord and in the power of His might. Put on the whole armor of God, that you may be able to stand against the Wiles of the devil. For we do not wrestle against flesh and blood, but against principalities, against powers, against the rulers of the darkness of this age, against spiritual hosts of wickedness in the heavenly places."

Verse ten begins with a command to "be strong." Please read this next sentence very carefully. Weak, powerless Christians do not please God. I know that is a startling statement but, dear saints, it is a true one. A weak, powerless Christian is one who not only embarrasses God, but gives Satan a license to devour and destroy everything in his life. Saint, God has called you to victory. And to ensure that you get it, He has given you His Spirit and His strength. If your strength is weak, I've got news for you -- God wants to give you His strength and power.

PRAYER = POWER

There is a tremendous revival of prayer sweeping over the entire earth. This is essential for God's end-time strategy for worldwide revival. Prayer produces power. God's power is purchased in the private place of prayer. A prayerless church is a powerless church. The prayerless Christian is a powerless Christian. Daniel 11:32 says that "the people who know their God shall be strong, and carry out great exploits." We know God through spending time with Him in prayer and, when we spend time with Him in prayer, we leave with His strength to do exploits.

To be an overcoming Christian in these last days is to be a

praying Christian. Hell has unleashed its greatest onslaught against mankind and against the Body of Christ. Dear believer, Satan hates you and is doing everything in his power to destroy you. God's counterattack is to clothe you with His armor and power to strike back at Satan's kingdom in the earth. We must pray to survive in these last days.

"Have you not known? Have you not heard? The everlasting God, the LORD, the Creator of the ends of the earth, neither faints nor is weary. His understanding is unsearchable. He gives power to the weak, and to those who have no might He increases strength. Even the youths shall faint and be weary, and the young men shall utterly fall, but those who wait on the LORD shall renew their strength; They shall mount up with wings like eagles, they shall run and not be weary, they shall walk and not faint." (Isaiah 40:28-31.)

SUBMIT TO GOD

Satan is at war with you, your family, your business, your church, your city, this nation and this world. He is a crazed renegade traitor and God's archenemy. He hates you because he hates God. God did not leave us without keys to aid us in our fight against Satan. 1 Peter 5:6-9 says "humble yourselves under the mighty hand of God, that He may exalt you in due time, casting all your care upon Him, for He cares for you. Be sober, be vigilant; because your adversary the devil walks about like a roaring lion, seeking whom he may devour. Resist him, steadfast in the faith, knowing that the same sufferings are experienced by your brotherhood in the world."

James 4:6-7 also says that "He gives more grace. Therefore He says: 'God resists the proud, But gives grace to the humble.' Therefore submit to God. Resist the devil and he will flee from you."

We humble ourselves to Him through prayer. We cast our cares upon Him through prayer. And we submit to God through prayer. After we do these things, we must realize it is God's will for us to resist, renounce and rebuke the devil and his forces from your life. God is ready to defeat all of His enemies in the earth in these last days. But God will only do that through His Body in the earth. Through us God longs to display His plan and power to all the earth.

KEYS TO THE KINGDOM

We've been given the keys to the kingdom of heaven in the earth - the keys to establish God's kingdom anywhere in the earth, the keys to destroy Satan's kingdom anywhere in the earth. Matthew 16:18-19 tells us: "And I also say to you that you are Peter, and on this rock I will build My church, and the gates of Hades shall not prevail against it. And I will give you the keys of the kingdom of heaven, and whatever you bind on earth will be bound in heaven, and whatever you loose on earth will be loosed in heaven."

In these days the gates of hell (Satan's authority over lives, families, cities and nations) shall not stop the offensive attack of the army of God in the earth. Through prayer we are seeing the gates of hell torn down all over the world.

IF WE WILL PRAY

God has bound Himself to the principle of prayer in the earth. God will not do anything in the earth, except in response to the prayers of His children. This is why we must pray. God has placed prayer at the very center of His involvement and activity.

God emphasizes this point in 2 Chronicles 7:14 when He said, "If my people, which are called by my name, shall humble themselves, and pray, and seek my face, and turn from their wicked ways; then will I hear from heaven, and will forgive their sin, and will heal their land."

If we as Christians will pray, God will respond by touching our nation. The Joshua Generation is a mighty prayer army releasing God's power to its families, cities and nations. There is a spirit of war in the Joshua Generation because God has declared war on His enemies.

God wants us to ask Him for the nations of the earth in this hour. " Ask of Me, and I will give You the nations for Your inheritance, and the ends of the earth for Your possession." (Psalm 2:8.) He is giving men and women all around the world a "city-taking spirit" in this time. For the first time in the history of the church, God has birthed this "city-taking spirit" in the hearts of literally thousands of His children. Why? Because He wants to invade our cities and nations with His love and life.

The word "possession" from Psalm 2:8 means "something seized." Satan and his army will not just let go of cities and nations because we want him to. He must be driven but by the power of God displayed through the Church. In this hour the praying church will display God's power in the earth -- "now the manifold wisdom of God might be made known by the church to the principalities and powers in the heavenly places." (Ephesians 3:10.) God is waiting on us. He is ready to reap the nations in a worldwide revival. He waits for us to see this and run to the place of prayer. The destiny of the entire world is in our hands. Let us seize the moment and see God's glory!

CHAPTER 4:
PEOPLE OF GOD'S WORD

God's Word is filled with God's life and power. His Word is the foundation of all we are and will be as Christians. All the success and victory for the believer comes from God's Word. In the same way, all our failures and defeats as Christians come from a lack of applying God's Word.

Joshua 1:7-8 highlights this fact when God tells Joshua to "only be strong and very courageous, that you may observe to do according to all the law which Moses My servant commanded you; do not turn from it to the right hand or to the left, that you may prosper wherever you go. This Book of the Law shall not depart from your mouth, but you shall meditate in it day and night, that you may observe to do according to all that is written in it. For then you will make your way prosperous, and then you will have good success."

In these two powerful verses, the Lord gives His guarantee

of success and victory for Joshua -- and for us, the Joshua
Generation. Three times in these two verses the lord promises
us "success" and "prosperity." He tells us that to the degree we
receive and obey His Word, we will live in His success.
Victory and success do not happen by accident. They happen
by choice. God's Word cannot fail. It will never pass away.

Hebrews 4:12 tells us that "the word of God is living and
powerful, and sharper than any two-edged sword,
piercing even to the division of soul and spirit, and of joints
and marrow, and is a Discerner of the thoughts and intents of
the heart."

So many Christians have been taught that life and
victory and answered prayers were the sole responsibility of
God. They have been taught that God, in His sovereign will,
chooses to bless, heal and help some, while at the same time,
He chooses to afflict and ignore others. Many times I have
heard believers say, with religious smugness, "It must be God's
will" when things go bad and victory is lost. But that is not
the case! God's Word is God's will. The choice is ours.

God has set before us life and death, blessing and cursing.
His Word brings life and blessing, but to reject or ignore His
Word is to choose death and cursing.

"But the word is very near you, in your mouth and in your
heart, that you may do it. 'See, I have set before you today
life and good, death and evil, in that I command you today to

love the LORD your God, to walk in His ways, and to keep His commandments, His statutes, and His judgments, that you may live and multiply; and the LORD your God will bless you in the land which you go to possess.

"But if your heart turns away so that you do not hear, and are drawn away, and worship other gods and serve them, I announce to you today that you shall surely perish; you shall not prolong your days in the land which you cross over the Jordan to go in and possess. I call heaven and earth as witnesses today against you, that I have set before you life and death, blessing and cursing; therefore choose life, that both you and your descendants may live; that you may love the LORD your God, that you may obey His voice, and that you may cling to Him, for He is your life and the length of your days; and that you may dwell in the land which the LORD swore to your fathers, to Abraham, Isaac, and Jacob, to give them.'" (Deuteronomy 30:14-20.)

SUCCESS IS NOT AN ACCIDENT

Success is not an accident; it is a choice. The Bible clearly lays out the things we need to do to be successful in life.

• **Respond to the Word of God.** Jesus taught us how to respond to the Word when he said, " 'Behold, a sower went out to sow. And as he sowed, some seed fell by the wayside;

and the birds came and devoured them. Some fell on stony places, where they did not have much earth; and they immediately sprang up because they had no depth of earth. But when the sun was up they were scorched, and because they had no root they withered away. And some fell among thorns, and the thorns sprang up and choked them. But others fell on good ground and yielded a crop: some a hundredfold, some sixty, some thirty…

"Therefore hear the parable of the sower: When anyone hears the word of the kingdom, and does not understand it, then the wicked one comes and snatches away what was sown in his heart. This is he who received seed by the wayside. But he who received the seed on stony places, this is he who hears the word and immediately receives it with joy; yet he has no root in himself, but endures only for a while. For when tribulation or persecution arises because of the word, immediately he stumbles. Now he who received seed among the thorns is he who hears the word, and the cares of this world and the deceitfulness of riches choke the word, and he becomes unfruitful. But he who received seed on the good ground is he who hears the word and understands it, who indeed bears fruit and produces: some a hundredfold, some sixty, some thirty.'" (Matthew 13:3-8, 18-23)

The seed of God's Word always produces when it is allowed to. The soil of our hearts must welcome and nurture the seed until it produces. It is not the fault of God's Word when we experience seed failure. It is the problem of our heart, our soul. The Joshua Generation is people who have put God's Word as first place in their lives.

• **Submit to the Word of God.**
Jesus said, "Blessed are the meek: for they shall inherit the earth." (Matthew 5:5) Jesus was telling us that to the degree we submit to God's Word, we will live in God's victory. He was saying, "Blessed are the teachable, for they shall be taught."

• **Value and Keep the Word of God.**
Psalm 1 gives us the picture of the man who values and keeps God's Word. "Blessed is the man who walks not in the counsel of the ungodly, nor stands in the path of sinners, nor sits in the seat of the scornful; but his delight is in the law of the LORD, and in His law he meditates day and night. He shall be like a tree planted by the rivers of water, that brings forth its fruit in its season, whose leaf also shall not wither; and whatever he does shall prosper." (Psalm 1:1-3.)

• **Fill Our Hearts and Minds with the Word of God.**
The Word of God brings success into our lives. When we

fill our hearts and minds with God's Word, God's Word will change us and produce God's nature in us. We read in Romans 12:2: "And do not be conformed to this world, but be transformed by the renewing of your mind, that you may prove what is that good and acceptable and perfect will of God."

- **Meditate on the Word of God.**
When we meditate day and night in God's Word, our lives become transformed. This transformation is the very purpose of God's Word. All of God's Word is filled with God's life and power, and will greatly benefit your life. According to 2 Timothy 3:16-17: "All Scripture is given by inspiration of God, and is profitable for doctrine, for reproof, for correction, for instruction in righteousness, that the man of God may be complete, thoroughly equipped for every good work."

- **Become Students and Disciples of the Word of God.**
To receive the full power and life of God's Word, we must become students and disciples of the Word. This is pointed out when Paul told Timothy to "be diligent to present yourself approved to God, a worker who does not need to be ashamed, rightly dividing the word of truth." (2 Timothy 2:15)

Jesus said this about being a disciple: "Then Jesus said to those Jews who believed Him, 'If you abide in My word, you are My disciples indeed. And you shall know the truth, and the truth shall make you free.'" (John 8:31-32) The disciple is one who "continues in God's Word." It is the disciple who knows the truth that sets him free. The casual, compromising Christian does not qualify as a disciple, and thus does not receive truth on a regular basis to bring freedom into his life.

The Joshua Generation is disciples of the Word of God. They honor and obey the Word of God and give it first place and priority in their lives.

CHAPTER 5:
PEOPLE OF LOVE

Two and a half of the tribes of the children of Israel received their inheritance before Israel had crossed the river. However, before they could settle down and enjoy their "promised land," they were commanded to help the other tribes cross over and receive their inheritance. This is a beautiful picture of the love God requires between believers. The twelve tribes maintained their individuality and distinction, but they were also bound together by being a nation.

In Joshua 1:12-15 we read: "And to the Reubenites, the Gadites, and half the tribe of Manasseh Joshua spoke, saying, 'Remember the word which Moses the servant of the LORD commanded you, saying, "The LORD your God is giving you rest and is giving you this land." Your wives, your little ones, and your livestock shall remain in the land which Moses gave you on this side of the Jordan. But you shall pass before your brethren armed, all your mighty men of valor, and help them, until the LORD has given your brethren rest, as He gave you, and they also have taken possession of the land which the LORD your God is giving them. Then you shall return to the land of your possession and enjoy it, which Moses the LORD's servant gave you on this side of the Jordan toward the sunrise.'"

Jesus said that the visible evidence that we are Christians is in a demonstration of love. "A new commandment I give to you, that you love one another; as I have loved you, that you also love one another. By this all will know that you are My disciples, if you have love for one another. By this shall all men know that ye are my disciples, if ye have love one to another." (John 13:34, 35)

Corrie Ten Boom once said "the Christian army is the only army in the world that shoots their wounded." She was referring to the judgmental attitude and the division that has filled much of the Church. It is time for us to love each other with the love of God that has been shed abroad in our hearts by the Holy Spirit. (Romans 5:5.)

1 John 4:16 tells us that "we have known and believed the love that God has for us. God is love, and he who abides in love abides in God, and God in him." God is love. Our Heavenly Father is love, and as His own children, we are filled

with His love. We are the children of perfect love. "Behold what manner of love the Father has bestowed on us, that we should be called children of God! Therefore the world does not know us, because it did not know Him." (1 John 3:1.)

God not only encourages us to love each other, He commands it. "Beloved, let us love one another, for love is of God; and everyone who loves is born of God and knows God. He who does not love does not know God, for God is love." (1 John 4:7, 8.)

The cruelest people I have ever known have been religious people. However, there is a vast difference between religion and relationship. The litmus test that we see here in 1 John is love. Love is the evidence that a person is truly born again. Jesus told us, "By their fruit you will know them." That fruit is found in a person's character and displayed in the way he treats other people.

HOW DO YOU TREAT OTHERS?

Jesus said, "Blessed are the merciful, for they shall obtain mercy." (Matthew 5:7) The Spirit of God opened this verse to me one day and said to me, "The way you treat other people is the same way God and people will treat you." It is true that whatever you sow, you will reap, as we see in Galatians 6:7, 8, which reads, "Do not be deceived, God is not mocked; for whatever a man sows, that he will also reap. For he who sows to his flesh will of the flesh reap corruption, but he who sows to the Spirit will of the Spirit reap everlasting life."

As you sow love and mercy into the lives of others, you will reap it back from both God and people. Jesus said, "Therefore, whatever you want men to do to you, do also to them, for this is the Law and the Prophets." (Matthew 7:12.)

This is the reality of that verse: what you make happen for others, God will make happen for you! I learned this life-changing truth at a critical point in the life of our church. I had felt God leading us to move from our leased church building, so I began to look around for a new, bigger building. During this time, although everything was going well with our church, we were not really growing, and we had no money to make the move to another bigger, more expensive building. While I was praying one day, the Lord told me to make happen for other's what I needed Him to do for me.

So, we began to give chairs, pulpits, sound systems, love offerings and other things to many churches and ministries. We were constantly looking for opportunities to sow into other churches.

About six months after sowing into other churches, we began to have a series of breakthroughs that ended up putting us into a brand new building.

The first Sunday in our new building we doubled the size

of our congregation. From there we kept growing. I constantly look for every opportunity to bless others because we've discovered the power of love.

Romans 13:8-10 tells us that we should "Owe no one anything except to love one another, for he who loves another has fulfilled the law. For the commandments, 'You shall not commit adultery,' 'You shall not murder,' 'You shall not steal,' 'You shall not bear false witness,' 'You shall not covet,' and if there is any other commandment, are all summed up in this saying, namely, 'You shall love your neighbor as yourself.' Love does no harm to a neighbor; therefore love is the fulfillment of the law."

Love is the fulfillment of the entire law. When you walk in God's love towards other people, you are pleasing God and acting like Him. "Therefore be imitators of God as dear children. And walk in love, as Christ also has loved us and given Himself for us, an offering and a sacrifice to God for a sweet-smelling aroma." (Ephesians 5:1, 2.)

GOD'S LOVE

In 1 Corinthians 13:1-8, 13 we have a very succinct description of God's love: "Though I speak with the tongues of men and of angels, but have not love, I have become sounding brass or a clanging cymbal. And though I have the gift of prophecy, and understand all mysteries and all knowledge, and though I have all faith, so that I could remove mountains, but have not love, I am nothing. And though I bestow all my goods to feed the poor, and though I give my body to be burned, but have not love, it profits me nothing.

"Love suffers long and is kind; love does not envy; love does not parade itself, is not puffed up; does not behave rudely, does not seek its own, is not provoked, thinks no evil; does not rejoice in iniquity, but rejoices in the truth; bears all things, believes all things, hopes all things, endures all things.

"Love never fails. But whether there are prophecies, they will fail; whether there are tongues, they will cease; whether there is knowledge, it will vanish away…And now abide faith, hope, love, these three; but the greatest of these is love."

The Joshua Generation is people who have made the quality decision to walk in love towards others.

God's love will never fail, and as we continue to sow His love in the lives of others, His love will produce a harvest of changed lives and healed hearts.

CHAPTER 6:
PEOPLE OF OBEDIENCE

The fifth principle of power found in Chapter One of
Joshua is the principle of obedience. It is the key to pleasing
to God.

In Joshua 1:16 we read: "So they answered Joshua, saying,
'All that you command us we will do, and wherever you send
us we will go. Just as we heeded Moses in all things, so we will
heed you. Only the LORD your God be with you, as He was
with Moses. Whoever rebels against your command and does
not heed your words, in all that you command him, shall be
put to death. Only be strong and of good courage.'"

We read in 1 Samuel 15:22-23: "So Samuel said: 'Has the
LORD as great delight in burnt offerings and sacrifices, as
in obeying the voice of the LORD? Behold, to obey is better
than sacrifice, and to heed than the fat of rams. For rebellion
is as the sin of witchcraft, and stubbornness is as iniquity and

idolatry. Because you have rejected the word of the LORD, He also has rejected you from being king.'"

God wants us to be obedient to Him. He is not impressed with personal sacrifices if they are a replacement for obedience to Him. Humility is the foundation of obedience. A humble person is not necessarily the one who drives the oldest car and wears the worst clothes, but true humility is manifest by obedience unto God. Micah 6:8 tells us that "He has shown you, O man, what is good; and what does the LORD require of you but to do justly, to love mercy, and to walk humbly with your God?"

Obedience is the product of humility and of meekness towards God. In James 4:6-7, God's Word tells us that "He gives more grace. Therefore He says: 'God resists the proud, But gives grace to the humble.' Therefore submit to God. Resist the devil and he will flee from you."

God is looking for obedience in our lives. "Likewise you younger people, submit yourselves to your elders. Yes, all of you be submissive to one another, and be clothed with humility, for 'God resists the proud, but gives grace to the humble.' Therefore humble yourselves under the mighty hand of God, that He may exalt you in due time, casting all your care upon Him, for He cares for you." (1 Peter 5:5, 6)

God resists the prideful. Pride is the worship of our own will and way. Pride is displayed by an unteachable spirit and leads to rebellion. Rebellion is to reject Godly authority. When a person becomes unteachable and rebellious, he opens the door to demonic influence and activity in his life. The prophet Isaiah warns us of this very thing: "'If you are willing and obedient, you shall eat the good of the land; but if you refuse and rebel, you shall be devoured by the sword'; For the mouth of the LORD has spoken." (Isaiah 1:19, 20.)

Pride is the source of rebellion, and rebellion produces demonic activity. Obedience is the product of humility, and obedience produces God's favor and blessing. God wants life to be well with you, and it will be well with you to the degree that you obey His Word. "Oh, that they had such a heart in them that they would fear Me and always keep all My commandments, that it might be well with them and with their children forever!" (Deuteronomy 5:29.)

God's authority in our lives begins with His Word. His Word is His will. His Word is His final authority. In His Word He also declares His government or authority in the earth. Ephesians 4:8-13 tells us, "'When He ascended on high, He led captivity captive, and gave gifts to men.' (Now this, 'He ascended' -- what does it mean but that He also first descended into the lower parts of the earth? He who descended is also the one who ascended far above all the heavens, that He might fill all things.)

And He Himself gave some to be apostles, some

prophets, some evangelists, and some pastors and teachers, for the equipping of the saints for the work of ministry, for the edifying of the Body of Christ, till we all come to the unity of the faith and of the knowledge of the Son of God, to a perfect man, to the measure of the stature of the fullness of Christ."

God has delegated authority to the five-fold government offices of the apostle, prophet, evangelist, pastor and teacher. These offices are given by God to lead, heal and equip God's people. Because God has anointed them and set them in their particular offices they carry a mantle from God. God expects His people to receive and be obedient under the mantle of these five offices. To rebel against these five God-anointed leaders is to rebel against God's authority structure in the earth and thus, to rebel against God Himself.

Hebrews 13:17 reads: "Obey those who rule over you, and be submissive, for they watch out for your souls, as those who must give account. Let them do so with joy and not with grief, for that would be unprofitable for you." Hebrews 13:7 also reads: "Remember those who rule over you, who have spoken the word of God to you, whose faith follow, considering the outcome of their conduct."

3 TYPES OF REBELLION

When you speak evil or act in rebellion toward a man of God, you have touched God with your rebellion. Psalm

105:14-15 tells us: "He permitted no one to do them wrong; yes, He rebuked kings for their sakes, saying, 'Do not touch My anointed ones, and do My prophets no harm.'" It is God who defends (and who also corrects) His anointed vessels.

For the church to be the army of God, we must obey and respect spiritual authority. The very foundation of military operation is the smooth flow and obedience in the chain of command. In God's system, every single person needs to be submitted to a local five-fold ministry. Any other way is to choose rebellion over obedience.

The Bible reveals three basic types of rebellion that the children of Israel faced.

1. The Rebellion of Ignorance and Immaturity.

In Numbers 14:1-4 we see this displayed: "So all the congregation lifted up their voices and cried, and the people wept that night. And all the children of Israel complained against Moses and Aaron, and the whole congregation said to them, 'If only we had died in the land of Egypt! Or if only we had died in this wilderness! Why has the LORD brought us to this land to fall by the sword, that our wives and children should become victims? Would it not be better for us to return to Egypt?' So they said to one another, 'Let us select a leader and return to Egypt.'"

Little children murmur about their parents when they

don't do what they want them to do. They have no real
understanding of life but are used to being taken care of.
This is also true of a baby Christian that murmurs because
the pastor forgot to shake his hand on Sunday, or because
everything is not going the way he thinks it should go.

This rebellion is the least serious (although all rebellion is
deadly), and God is the most lenient when His children are
in this type of rebellion. The same way a parent drives
rebellion from his children, God will drive rebellion from
His. Correction is the answer to the rebellion of ignorance
and immaturity. When you begin to grow as a Christian,
you soon leave the place where this kind of rebellion is
tolerable to God. Don't point the finger of accusation and
blame at God's man and God if everything doesn't go
exactly right for you. Grow up and go on in God!

2. The Rebellion of Familiarity.
The second type of rebellion found in the children of Israel
is the rebellion of familiarity as found in Numbers 12:1-
2: "Then Miriam and Aaron spoke against Moses because
of the Ethiopian woman whom he had married; for he
had married an Ethiopian woman. So they said, "Has the
LORD indeed spoken only through Moses? Has He not
spoken through us also?" And the LORD heard it."

Because Miriam and Aaron were close to Moses, they saw

him in his humanness and frailty. Satan planted seeds of rebellion, and they said to Moses, "We can hear from God as well as you can!"

Listen, dear believer, just because God has used you in the gifts or to do something great for Him, doesn't mean you are suddenly on a spiritual par with your pastor. When you begin to act like that, the Bible says in verse 2 of the above, "And the Lord heard it." God hears your rebellion against His leaders, and it brings His judgment. When God allows you to be close to a man of God and to see his weakness, remember this, that it is God's mantle and anointing in that person that sets him apart, not his fleshly abilities.

3. The Rebellion of Pride.

The third and deadliest kind of rebellion found in the children of Israel is the rebellion of pride. "Now Korah the son of Izhar, the son of Kohath, the son of Levi, with Dathan and Abiram the sons of Eliab, and On the son of Peleth, sons of Reuben, took men; and they rose up before Moses with some of the children of Israel, two hundred and fifty leaders of the congregation, representatives of the congregation, men of renown. They gathered together against Moses and Aaron, and said to them, "You take too much upon yourselves, for all the congregation is holy, every one of them, and the LORD is among them. Why then do you exalt yourselves above the assembly of the LORD?" So when Moses heard it, he fell on his face...." (Numbers 16:1-4.)

One of the princes of Israel, Korah, rose up against God's man, Moses, and said to him, "Who put you in charge here?" Korah questioned Moses' right and authority as a leader, and suggested that there was other more qualified leaders in the camp (like himself). Korah, whose name means "cold and uncovered," was an example of the worst kind of rebellion, that which is spread in the heart of leaders. This rebellion of leadership is the direct product of the spirit of Lucifer.

Lucifer (Satan's name before his fall from heaven) was God's most beautiful creation. He led the choir of heaven in praise around the throne of God. But iniquity was found in his heart, and he rebelled against God. "How you are fallen from heaven, O Lucifer, son of the morning! How you are cut down to the ground, you who weakened the nations! For you have said in your heart: 'I will ascend into heaven, I will exalt my throne above the stars of God; I will also sit on the mount of the congregation on the farthest sides of the north; I will ascend above the heights of the clouds, I will be like the Most High.' Yet you shall be brought down to Sheol, to the lowest depths of the Pit." (Isaiah 14:12-15.)

Lucifer, who rose up in rebellion against God, was the

cause of the first "church split" in heaven. The spirit of Lucifer is that rebellious spirit that tries to attack leaders in the Body of Christ. Satan can do no real damage to a church unless he deceives and manipulates a leader to do it.

Korah not only rose up in rebellion, he also got two hundred and fifty other prominent leaders to side with him. This rebellion of a leader isn't satisfied by just leaving. It wants to take all the people with it! To enter or follow this rebellion is to uncover yourself spiritually. Ecclesiastes 10:8 tells us that "he who digs a pit will fall into it, and whoever breaks through a wall will be bitten by a serpent."

God severely judges this rebellion of pride because of its devastating effects in the Body of Christ. The earth opened up and swallowed Korah and his men alive, and this kind of rebellion will swallow you alive if you enter into it. There is no such thing as a good church split. Division is always the product of Satan and rebellion in the hearts of men.

The Joshua Generation is people submitted and committed to each other and God's authority.

You can conquer rebellion by clothing yourself in humility and by having an obedient spirit. Obedience is the key to pleasing God!

CHAPTER 7:
TAKING OUR FAMILES FOR GOD

In the second chapter of the book of Joshua, we see that Rahab had hidden the two spies from the king's men, and because she helped them, they responded to her plea to protect her family when the city would be taken. The two spies are a type of GOD'S PROMISES concerning the salvation of your family. God wants you to hide in your heart His Word concerning your family, just like Rahab hid the spies in her house. Rahab's name means "spaciously enlarged." Rahab's heart was "spaciously enlarged" to ask and then see the salvation of her entire family. She wasn't content with her own salvation, but her desire was for her whole family to be saved.

We read in Joshua 2:12-13, 18: "'Now therefore, I beg you, swear to me by the LORD, since I have shown you kindness, that you also will show kindness to my father's house, and give me a true token, and spare my father, my mother, my brothers, my sisters, and all that they have, and deliver our lives from death'"…So the men said to her: "'We will be blameless of this oath of yours which you have made us swear, unless, when we come into the land, you bind this line of scarlet cord in the window through which you let us down, and unless you bring your father, your mother, your brothers, and all your father's household to your own home.'"

The Lord spoke to me about our families as believers. He told me that He was bringing a revival of salvation and answered prayers concerning the lost family members of His children. He told me that we would see a great harvest of our families into the Kingdom of God.

The first step to seeing all of your family brought into the Kingdom of God is to believe it is God's will to save them. As long as Satan's deceiving voice is whispering in your ear that "it must not be God's will to save them" or "they have their own will" or some other lie, you will never pray in faith long enough to see God work in their lives. It is the will of God for your family to be saved!

The Word of God says that if we believe, we will be saved "and our house." God wants you to believe that He wants to save your family. "'Who will tell you words by which you and all your household will be saved.'" (Acts 11:14.) Read that again: "All your house will be saved." Has Satan been robbing your faith and ripping off your family? Now is the time for you to stand and claim what is your God-given right and responsibility to see your family saved.

The scripture is full of entire families being saved.

- "Then Crispus, the ruler of the synagogue, believed on the Lord with all his household. And many of the Corinthians, hearing, believed and were baptized." (Acts 18:8.)

- "But at midnight Paul and Silas were praying and singing hymns to God, and the prisoners were listening to them. Suddenly there was a great earthquake, so that the foundations of the prison were shaken; and immediately all the doors were opened and everyone's chains were loosed.

  "And the keeper of the prison, awaking from sleep and seeing the prison doors open, supposing the prisoners had fled, drew his sword and was about to kill himself. "But Paul called with a loud voice, saying, 'Do yourself no harm, for we are all here.' Then he called for a light, ran in, and fell down trembling before Paul and Silas. And he brought them out and said, 'Sirs, what must I do to be saved?' So they said, 'Believe on the Lord Jesus Christ, and you will be saved, you and your household.' Then they spoke the word of the Lord to him and to all who were in his house." (Acts 16:25-32.)

- "So the father knew that it was at the same hour in which Jesus said to him, 'Your son lives.' And he himself believed, and his whole household." (John 4:53.)

SATAN'S BLINDING INFLUENCE

For too many years we've let Satan rob members of our families because we weren't sure if it was "God's will" for them to be saved, or because we were taught about their "free will." Unsaved people do not have a "free will," but instead they are prisoners of the power of Satan. They are blinded by his deception, and until someone breaks that bondage off of them, they will stay unsaved.

Paul, in his letter to the Corinthians, says, "But even if our Gospel is veiled, it is veiled to those who are perishing, whose minds the god of this age has blinded, who do not believe, lest the light of the Gospel of the glory of Christ, who is the image of God, should shine on them." (2 Corinthians 4:3, 4.)

This understanding of Satan's blinding influence among the unsaved is at the very center of God's plan for us to see our families saved and delivered. You see, dear saint, there are evil spirits from hell assigned to your family members, and they will rob, kill and destroy your loved ones and keep them out of heaven until you or another believer stops them.

There is a scriptural key to understanding the operation of Satan's influence in your family. That key can be found in several scriptures:

- "You shall not bow down to them nor serve them. For I, the LORD your God, am a jealous God, visiting the iniquity of the fathers upon the children to the third and fourth generations of those who hate Me, but showing mercy to thousands, to those who love Me and keep My commandments." (Deuteronomy 5:9, 10.)

- "The LORD is longsuffering and abundant in mercy, forgiving iniquity and transgression; but He by no means clears the guilty, visiting the iniquity of the fathers on the children to the third and fourth generation." (Numbers 14:18.)

- "You shall not bow down to them nor serve them. For I, the LORD your God, am a jealous God, visiting the iniquity of the fathers upon the children to the third and fourth generations of those who hate Me...." (Exodus 20:5.)

- "Keeping mercy for thousands, forgiving iniquity and transgression and sin, by no means clearing the guilty, visiting the iniquity of the fathers upon the children and the children's children to the third and the fourth generation." (Exodus 34:7.)

• "You show lovingkindness to thousands, and repay the iniquity of the fathers into the bosom of their children after them -- the Great, the Mighty God, whose name is the LORD of hosts." (Jeremiah 32:18.)

Going back to Deuteronomy 5:9-10 we read: "You shall not bow down to them nor serve them. For I, the LORD your God, am a jealous God, visiting the iniquity of the fathers upon the children to the third and fourth generations of those who hate Me, but showing mercy to thousands, to those who love Me and keep My commandments." This scripture tells us that there is a "passing on" of sin and iniquity to the third and fourth generation of a family bloodline. Sin is not a biological problem, but instead it is a spiritual one. The way that it is passed down in a family is by family spirits.

As a pastor, I have seen this principle of family spirits manifest in many families. For example, the woman whose grandmother died of cancer, whose mother died of cancer, and who now has been told that she has cancer. How did she get cancer? By the passing down of a family spirit! Or what about the man who is an alcoholic, whose father was an alcoholic, and whose grandfather was an alcoholic? It is a family spirit! This evil family inheritance can be broken by the Blood of Jesus Christ. You can remove and free your family from family spirits.

God wants us to fight for our families in the spirit. Nehemiah echoes this in Nehemiah 4:14: "And I looked, and arose and said to the nobles, to the leaders, and to the rest of the people, 'Do not be afraid of them. Remember the Lord, great and awesome, and fight for your brethren, your sons, your daughters, your wives, and your houses.'" Nehemiah told God's people to "FIGHT FOR YOUR FAMILIES." Paul also tells us to "be strong in the Lord and in the power of His might. Put on the whole armor of God that you may be able to stand against the Wiles of the devil. For we do not wrestle against flesh and blood, but against principalities, against powers, against the rulers of the darkness of this age, against spiritual hosts of wickedness in the heavenly places." (Ephesians 6:10-12.)

ENLARGE OUR HEARTS

God enlarged Rahab's heart to ask and believe for the salvation of her family. May God enlarge our hearts to ask and believe and fight for our loved ones!

Jesus taught about overcoming the strongholds of the enemy in Luke 11:20-22: "But if I cast out demons with the finger of God, surely the kingdom of God has come upon you. When a strong man, fully armed, guards his own palace, his goods are in peace. But when a stronger than he comes upon him and overcomes him, he takes from him all his armor in which he trusted, and divides his spoils."

By His Name and Blood, Jesus has given us authority over Satan's power in the earth. We read in Luke 10:19: "Behold, I give unto you power to tread on serpents and scorpions, and over all the power of the enemy: and nothing shall by any means hurt you."

Just as Rahab let down a "scarlet thread" so must we claim the salvation and deliverance of our families by the Blood of Jesus. The Blood of Jesus is God's covenant commitment to us for our and our families' salvation. Also, in Revelation 12:11 we read: "And they overcame him by the blood of the Lamb and by the word of their testimony, and they did not love their lives to the death."

The Joshua Generation is believers who are taking their families for God. They are rebuking and binding Satan's power over their families. And their confession is the same as Joshua's: "And if it seems evil to you to serve the LORD, choose for yourselves this day whom you will serve, whether the gods which your fathers served that were on the other side of the River, or the gods of the Amorites, in whose land you dwell. But as for me and my house, we will serve the LORD." (Joshua 24:15.)

CHAPTER 8:
FOLLOWING THE ARK: THE RESTORATION OF THE FIVE-FOLD MINISTRY

"Then Joshua rose early in the morning; and they set out from Acacia Grove and came to the Jordan, he and all the children of Israel, and lodged there before they crossed over.

"So it was, after three days, that the officers went through the camp; and they commanded the people, saying, 'When you see the ark of the covenant of the LORD your God, and the priests, the Levites, bearing it, then you shall set out from your place and go after it. Yet there shall be a space between you and it, about two thousand cubits by measure. Do not come near it, that you may know the way by which you must go, for you have not passed this way before.'

"And Joshua said to the people, 'Sanctify yourselves, for tomorrow the LORD will do wonders among you.' Then Joshua spoke to the priests, saying, 'Take up the ark of the

70 \\ CHAPTER 8: FOLLOWING THE ARK

covenant and cross over before the people.' So they took up the Ark of the Covenant and went before the people." (Joshua 3:1-6.)

God is restoring to His church anointed, godly and called ministers. They are carrying "the ark" of His presence before the people of God. They are teaching God's people, and leading them by example into the Promised Land of God's perfect will. They are bringing God's people across the Jordan. The Jordan is a type of fleshly limitations. God's anointed ministers are leading the people of God over the river of fleshly limitations into the life of the Spirit.

The Joshua Generation will walk and live in the Spirit. They will stay filled with the Spirit.

Ephesians 4:11-13 tells us about the five-fold ministry: "And He Himself gave some to be apostles, some prophets, some evangelists, and some pastors and teachers, for the equipping of the saints for the work of ministry, for the edifying of the Body of Christ Every believer must be under the guidance and covering that God has provided through the five-fold ministry. We are witnessing the emergence of a "new breed" of leader in the earth. For the first time in the history of the Church, God has put in the heart of literally thousands of ministers to take their cities for God, and even to take their nation for God. They are teaching and preaching "fresh manna" from heaven to their congregations.

God has placed the desire to be under a Godly pastor in the heart of every believer. Find a Godly pastor, and learn and grow under his leadership.

The priesthood was to go first over the Jordan. A leader cannot lead others when he hasn't gone first himself. He can't feed others what he hasn't eaten as a leader.

The people were to keep a space between them and the priesthood. That space is a type of respect and honor that God's people are to give to the ministry. Your pastor is not "your buddy." You should not call him by his first name alone. Honor him as your "pastor" when you speak to him. When the distance between the leader and the people disappears, so does the respect that God requires of His people. To be a minister, you can't be everyone's best friend and pal. You must honor the anointing God gave you and respect it.

The leaders of Israel communicated to the vast congregation of Israelites with the sound of a trumpet. This trumpet is a type of the current voice and leading of the Holy Spirit spoken through anointed ministry. The sound of the trumpet is a type of prophetic word that God speaks to His people. "Cry aloud, spare not; lift up your voice like a trumpet; tell My people their transgression, and the house of Jacob their sins." (Isaiah 58:1.) God is trumpeting a distinct voice and direction to His people today. "Also, I set watchmen over you, saying, 'Listen to the sound of the trumpet!'" (Jeremiah 6:17.)

We see the great importance of the ministry to lead and warn God's people in Ezekiel 33:4-7: "'When whoever hears the sound of the trumpet and does not take warning, if the sword comes and takes him away, his blood shall be on his own head. He heard the sound of the trumpet, but did not take warning; his blood shall be upon himself. But he who takes warning will save his life. But if the watchman sees the sword coming and does not blow the trumpet, and the people are not warned, and the sword comes and takes any person from among them, he is taken away in his iniquity; but his blood I will require at the watchman's hand.' So you, son of man: I have made you a watchman for the house of Israel; therefore you shall hear a word from My mouth and warn them for Me."

Jesus said seven times in the Gospels, as well as seven times in the book of Revelation, "He that hath ears to hear, let him hear."

FIVE REASONS FOR BLOWING THE TRUMPET

There were five reasons for blowing the trumpet in the camp of the children of Israel. These five reasons are five distinct directions that God is speaking through His leadership to the people of God today. In Numbers 10:1-3, "the LORD spoke to Moses, saying: 'Make two silver trumpets for yourself; you shall make them of hammered work; you shall use them for calling the congregation and for directing the movement of the camps.'"

1. Unity

The first purpose for blowing the trumpet was for **UNITY**, to call the whole assembly together. God is blowing the trumpet of unity to the Body of Christ today. Unity is a requirement for revival.

Numbers 10:3 says, "When they blow both of them, all the congregation shall gather before you at the door of the tabernacle of meeting." God reiterates this in Psalm 133:1: "Behold, how good and how pleasant it is for brethren to dwell together in unity! It is like the precious oil upon the head, running down on the beard, the beard of Aaron, running down on the edge of his garments. It is like the dew of Hermon, descending upon the mountains of Zion; for there the LORD commanded the blessing -- life forevermore."

Unity always begins at the top and flows down. Unity comes into a church when the leaders are in unity. It comes to a home when the parents are in unity. Jesus prayed that you and I would come into unity: "I do not pray for these alone, but also for those who will believe in Me through their word; that they all may be one, as You, Father, are in Me, and I in You; that they also may be one in Us, that the world may believe that You sent Me. And the glory which You gave Me I have given them, that they may be one just as We are one: I in them, and You in Me; that they may be made perfect in one, and that the world may know that You have sent Me, and have loved them as You have loved Me." (John 17:20–23.)

Let us come together as one great army of God and see God's glory fill our land! "But if they blow only one, then the leaders, the heads of the divisions of Israel, shall gather to you." (Numbers 10:4.)

2. Leadership

The second reason for blowing the trumpet was to gather the **LEADERSHIP** of Israel together. God is calling leaders to come together and seek God. We see this in action in the Book of Acts where the Holy Spirit spoke to leaders as they gathered together. "Now in the church that was at Antioch there were certain prophets and teachers: Barnabas, Simeon who was called Niger, Lucius of Cyrene, Manaen who had been brought up with Herod the tetrarch, and Saul. As they ministered to the Lord and fasted, the Holy Spirit said, "Now separate to Me Barnabas and Saul for the work to which I have called them.'"

God is calling the leaders of local churches, cities and nations together so He can speak to them and empower them for the new direction He has for His people. If you are a leader, hear this trumpet! Gather and fellowship with other leaders, and receive God's instructions for taking our cities for God. "But if they blow only one, then the leaders, the heads of the divisions of Israel, shall gather to you." (Numbers 10:4.)

3. Advancement

We find that the third reason for blowing the trumpet was for God's whole congregation to **MOVE ON** or **AD-VANCE.** When the cloud or fire of God's presence moved, it was up to the leadership to blow the trumpet and move God's people with God. When God moves, we must move.

The Joshua Generation follows the presence of God and moves when God moves.

Today we are seeing a separation of the Body of Christ. God is moving on, and many people don't want to move from where they are. They've become comfortable and have not wanted to change. Over the past four decades we have seen a **PROGRESSIVE MOVE** of God in the earth. God restored praise and worship. Then He restored faith, and we received great blessings from the principles of faith. However, many didn't move with God into the arena of faith. They didn't hear or respond to the trumpet blast to move on. In fact, many have preached and have taught against "moving on" into the new things of God. Even today, many are speaking against the "prophetic move" and the "kingdom move." But, child of God, don't fight what God is doing in the earth! Yes, change can be unsettling and difficult, but the Christian life is a journey and lifestyle to change.

You must realize that when you stop changing and moving with God, you lose the freshness and power of His presence. Jesus defined the life of a Christian in John 8:31-32: "Then Jesus said to those Jews who believed Him, 'If you abide in My word, you are My disciples indeed. And you shall know the truth, and the truth shall make you free.'" A disciple is one who continues in God's word. He has disciplined himself to live and obey God's Word. Jesus said that it is this kind of person, this disciple, to whom the truth comes, and the truth will set you free! Truth is not cheap. It is the reward of discipleship.

4. War

"When you go to war in your land against the enemy who oppresses you, then you shall sound an alarm with the trumpets, and you will be remembered before the LORD your God, and you will be saved from your enemies." (Numbers 10:9.)

The fourth reason for sounding the trumpet is to call the people to **WAR**. This trumpet sound was an alarm that woke the entire nation for the purpose of battle. An example of this can be found in Joel 2:1, 7-11; 3:9-10.

First, in Joel 2:1, 7-11: "Blow the trumpet in Zion, and sound an alarm in My holy mountain! Let all the inhabitants of the land tremble; for the day of the LORD is coming, for it is at hand…They run like mighty men, they climb the wall like men of war; every one marches in formation, and they do not break ranks. They do not push one another; every one marches in his own column. Though they lunge between the weapons, they are not cut down. They run to and fro in the city, they run on the wall; they climb into the houses, they enter at the windows like a thief. The earth quakes before them, the heavens tremble; the sun and moon grow dark, and the stars diminish their brightness. The LORD gives voice before His army, for His camp is very great; for strong is the one who executes His word. for the day of the LORD is great and very terrible; who can endure it?"

And in Joel 3:9-10 we read: "Proclaim this among the nations: 'Prepare for war! Wake up the mighty men, let all the men of war draw near, let them come up. Beat your plowshares into swords And your pruning hooks into spears; let the weak say, 'I am strong.'"

God is calling His Church to war. It is time for war in the Body of Christ! "For though we walk in the flesh, we do not war according to the flesh. For the weapons of our warfare are not carnal but mighty in God for pulling down strongholds, casting down arguments and every high thing that exalts itself against the knowledge of God, bringing every thought into captivity to the obedience of Christ." (2 Corinthians 10:4-5.)

If, as God's ministers in the land, we don't sound the trumpet of war, then we have surrendered God's people to be taken captive by the enemy. We are led to this great battle by our Commander-in-Chief, the Lord Jesus Christ.

He said in Matthew 16:18-19: "And I also say to you that you are Peter, and on this rock I will build My church, and the gates of Hades shall not prevail against it. And I will give you the keys of the kingdom of heaven, and whatever you bind on earth will be bound in heaven, and whatever you loose on earth will be loosed in heaven."

We have been given the keys to tear down the gates of hell. The reason that I have become a warrior is because if I don't war, who will fight for my family, my wife, my church, my city and my nation? "Speak to the children of Israel, and say to them: 'When you have crossed the Jordan into the land of Canaan, then you shall drive out all the inhabitants of the land from before you, destroy all their engraved stones, destroy all their molded images, and demolish all their high places; you shall dispossess the inhabitants of the land and dwell in it, for I have given you the land to possess. And you shall divide the land by lot as an inheritance among your families; to the larger you shall give a larger inheritance, and to the smaller you shall give a smaller inheritance; there everyone's inheritance shall be whatever falls to him by lot. You shall inherit according to the tribes of your fathers. But if you do not drive out the inhabitants of the land from before you, then it shall be that those whom you let remain shall be irritants in your eyes and thorns in your sides, and they shall harass you in the land where you dwell. Moreover it shall be that I will do to you as I thought to do to them.'" (Numbers 33:51-56)

If you refuse the trumpet of war because "I don't know about that warfare stuff" or "I don't feel called to spiritual warfare," then you have surrendered to defeat by your inactivity. "For if the trumpet makes an uncertain sound, who will prepare for battle?" (1 Corinthians 14:8.) The trumpet has sounded, rise up, O Mighty Army of God!

5. Call to Worship God

The fifth reason for the trumpet being blown was to call the children of Israel together to praise and worship God. It was a **CALL TO WORSHIP GOD.** Numbers 10:10 reads: "Also in the day of your gladness, in your appointed feasts, and at the beginning of your months, you shall blow the trumpets over your burnt offerings and over the sacrifices of your peace offerings; and they shall be a memorial for you before your God: I am the LORD your God."

Today, there is a revival of praise and worship sweeping over the whole earth. There are more people praising God right now than there has been in the history of the human race.

Father God seeks worshippers in the earth. Jesus said that "the hour is coming, and now is, when the true worshipers will worship the Father in spirit and truth; for the Father is seeking such to worship Him. God is Spirit, and those who worship Him must worship in spirit and truth." (John 5:23, 24.) God has always preceded His great moves in the earth with worship and praise. When Jesus was born, the heavenly choir sang the praises of God. Jesus is coming soon for a worshipping Bride in the earth. "For we are the circumcision, who worship God in the Spirit, rejoice in Christ Jesus, and have no confidence in the flesh...." (Philippians 3:3.)

Our priestly ministry to God is not in natural priestly

duties, but in spiritual sacrifices of praise and worship. "Rejoice in the LORD always. And again I will say, rejoice!" (Philippians 4:4.) We are to live in an environment of praise towards God! It is God's will for you to stay filled with His Spirit by keeping a song in your heart.

"See then that you walk circumspectly, not as fools but as wise, redeeming the time, because the days are evil. Therefore do not be unwise, but understand what the will of the Lord is. And do not be drunk with wine, in which is dissipation; but be filled with the Spirit, speaking to one another in psalms and hymns and spiritual songs, singing and making melody in your heart to the Lord, giving thanks always for all things to God the Father in the name of our Lord Jesus Christ...." (Ephesians 5:15-20.)

God is leading His people by the prophetic teaching, preaching and direction of anointed ministers.

The Joshua Generation is marching together in unity, following their Captain and Commander, Jesus Christ.

CHAPTER 9:
THE ROCK OF REVELATION

The Book of Joshua is a military manual on how to take our cities for God. Its language, examples and typology are all filled with wisdom and strategy to be God's conquering people in the earth. We read in 1 Corinthians 10:11: "Now all these things happened unto them for examples: and they are written for our admonition, upon whom the ends of the world are come."

I believe God has given us the Book of Joshua for the end-time church, for the Joshua Generation. Allow the Holy Spirit to breathe life and revelation into your spirit and stir you for the greatest time of the church and of human history.

The fourth chapter of Joshua details God's instructions for a leader from every one of the twelve tribes to take a stone out of the middle of the Jordan River. These stones were to be taken to dry land and made into a memorial of God's victory in stopping the river for them.

"And it came to pass, when all the people had completely crossed over the Jordan, that the LORD spoke to Joshua, saying: 'Take for yourselves twelve men from the people, one man from every tribe, and command them, saying, "Take for yourselves twelve stones from here, out of the midst of the Jordan, from the place where the priests' feet stood firm. You shall carry them over with you and leave them in the lodging place where you lodge tonight."'" (Joshua 4:1-7.)

The twelve stones speak to us of the rock of revelation knowledge and its foundation place in the life of the believer. God has brought great revelation to the church in the past few decades. The church of this generation is the most taught and equipped church in history. With this great blessing comes a great responsibility. God expects a return on His investment of revelation. He expects us to rise up as the end-time army of God, and to conquer His enemies in the earth. Revelation knowledge is the very foundation of the church. Jesus illuminates this in Matthew 16:15-19: "He said to them, 'But who do you say that I am?' Simon Peter answered and said, 'You are the Christ, the Son of the living God.' Jesus answered and said to him, 'Blessed are you, Simon Bar-Jonah, for flesh and blood has not revealed this to you, but My Father who is in heaven. And I also say to you that you are Peter, and on this rock I will build My church, and the gates of Hades shall not prevail against it.'"

Jesus asked Simon, "Who do you say that I am?" That is still the central question in the heart of all people. Who is Jesus to you? Jesus said that the Father had revealed to Simon who Jesus was (the Christ, the Son of God). Of course, Jesus is the cornerstone of Christianity, but in order to see who He is, it takes revelation knowledge from God. So, this process of revelation precedes truth and understanding.

Something powerful happened when Simon received revelation knowledge. His very character and nature were changed. Simon means "a reed." A reed is blown with every breeze. It has no stability or strength. God doesn't call strong people. He makes the weak people strong. Jesus changed Simon's name to Peter, which means "a rock." Revelation will change your nature from "a reed" to "a rock."

Jesus said He would build His church upon this rock of revelation knowledge, with He, Himself, being the chief cornerstone. This foundation of rock is a type of apostolic teaching. We read in Ephesians 2:19-22: "Now, therefore, you are no longer strangers and foreigners, but fellow citizens with the saints and members of the household of God, having been built on the foundation of the apostles and prophets, Jesus Christ Himself being the chief cornerstone, in whom the whole building, being fitted together, grows into a holy temple in the Lord, in whom you also are being built together for a dwelling place of God in the Spirit."

This apostolic teaching is the foundation of the New Testament church. Many Christians today are confused and deceived because they've been sidetracked by some "funny doctrine" or teaching that they have received. Many Christians are having "foundation trouble" in their lives because they never had a proper foundation laid down. Dear saint, apostolic doctrine is that which is foundational and primary to the believer. In Ephesians 4:11-14 we read: "And He Himself gave some to be apostles, some prophets, some evangelists, and some pastors and teachers, for the equipping of the saints for the work of ministry, for the edifying of the Body of Christ, till we all come to the unity of the faith and of the knowledge of the Son of God, to a perfect man, to the measure of the stature of the fullness of Christ; that we should no longer be children, tossed to and fro and carried about with every wind of doctrine, by the trickery of men, in the cunning craftiness of deceitful plotting...."

Today, many self-appointed and self-anointed teachers have seduced God's people with "winds of doctrine" and "cunning craftiness." They have majored in the minors, and have brought division and deception to God's people. The Bible warns us about this in 1 Timothy 4:1-3: "Now the Spirit expressly says that in latter times some will depart from the faith, giving heed to deceiving spirits and doctrines of demons, speaking lies in hypocrisy, having their own conscience seared with a hot iron, forbidding to marry, and commanding to abstain from foods which God created to be received with thanksgiving by those who believe and know the truth."

We also read about the last days in 2 Timothy 4:2-4: "Preach the word! Be ready in season and out of season. Convince, rebuke, exhort, with all longsuffering and teaching. For the time will come when they will not endure sound doctrine, but according to their own desires, because they have itching ears, they will heap up for themselves teachers; and they will turn their ears away from the truth, and be turned aside to fables."

God is bringing the church back to the basics. The phenomenon of "itching ears" is descriptive of much of the activity of the charismatic movement during the past few years. Teachers and preachers had a "Can you top this?" attitude. The desire for the spectacular and for "heavy revy" teaching sidetracked God's people from the soundness and simplicity of the Gospel. For example, it is more important in God's eyes for you to love your wife or husband and family, than to understand the secrets of the book of Revelation perfectly.

I encourage you to find a pastor (if you don't already have one) who will teach you the principle doctrines of Jesus Christ. Jesus said, "Therefore whoever hears these sayings of

Mine, and does them, I will liken him to a wise man who built his house on the rock: and the rain descended, the floods came, and the winds blew and beat on that house; and it did not fall, for it was founded on the rock. But everyone who hears these sayings of Mine, and does not do them, will be like a foolish man who built his house on the sand: and the rain descended, the floods came, and the winds blew and beat on that house; and it fell. And great was its fall." (Matthew 4:24-27.)

The "prophecy teacher" on television will not counsel you when your family faces a battle. He will not pray for your sick children. Also, "fluff" teaching will not help you endure the storms of life. The sound, basic teaching of the doctrines of Christ and the Kingdom of God will help you overcome and be a victorious, successful Christian.

CHAPTER 10:
CONQUERING CANAAN: THE SEVEN ENEMIES OF THE JOSHUA GENERATION

It must have sounded strange at first when God said to the children of Israel, "I have a promised land for you. It is a place of victory and provision and peace. It is your inheritance as My children. And oh, by the way, there are seven nations greater and fiercer than you there, and I would like you to drive them out of your land." The first generation said, "We'll pass on that one, God." They chose to die in the desert rather than to face their enemies. However, there arose another generation of leaders and people that had a "possessing mentality." They would not he denied their God-given inheritance!

"When the LORD your God brings you into the land which you go to possess, and has cast out many nations before you, the Hittites and the Girgashites and the Amorites and the Canaanites and the Perizzites and the Hivites and the Jebusites, seven nations greater and mightier than you, and when the LORD your God delivers them over to you, you shall conquer them and utterly destroy them. You shall make no covenant with them nor show mercy to them. Nor shall you make marriages with them. You shall not give your daughter to their son, nor take their daughter for your son. For they will turn your sons away from following Me, to serve other gods; so the anger of the LORD will be aroused against you and destroy you suddenly. But thus you shall deal with them: you shall destroy their altars, and break down their sacred pillars, and cut down their wooden images, and burn their carved images with fire.

"For you are a holy people to the LORD your God; the LORD your God has chosen you to be a people for Himself, a special treasure above all the peoples on the face of the earth." (Deuteronomy 7:1-6.)

These seven tribes are all types of the seven enemies of the Joshua Generation. The greatest struggles the church must face before she inherits her place of victory and prosperity are internal, not external. Before we can truly live in our Promised Land and change the world for God, we must individually, and then corporately, defeat and drive out of our lives these seven greatest enemies.

We find these seven enemies in Deuteronomy 20:16-18:

"But of the cities of these peoples which the LORD your God gives you as an inheritance, you shall let nothing that breathes remain alive, but you shall utterly destroy them: the Hittite and the Amorite and the Canaanite and the Perizzite and the Hivite and the Jebusite, just as the LORD your God has commanded you, lest they teach you to do according to all their abominations which they have done for their gods, and you sin against the LORD your God."

The Lord knows the destructive power of compromise, and He has commanded us to live uncompromisingly before Him. The compromising Christian is the one who refuses to confront and conquer those enemies of God. Compromise always brings defeat in our lives, and it also offends God.

"Speak to the children of Israel, and say to them: 'When you have crossed the Jordan into the land of Canaan, then you shall drive out all the inhabitants of the land from before you, destroy all their engraved stones, destroy all their molded images, and demolish all their high places; you shall dispossess the inhabitants of the land and dwell in it, for I have given you the land to possess. And you shall divide the land by lot as an inheritance among your families; to the larger you shall give a larger inheritance, and to the smaller you shall give a smaller inheritance; there everyone's inheritance shall be whatever falls to him by lot. You shall inherit according to the tribes of your fathers. But if you do not drive out the inhabitants of the land from before you, then it shall be that those whom you let remain shall be irritants in your eyes and thorns in your sides, and they shall harass you in the land where you dwell. Moreover it shall be that I will do to you as I thought to do to them.'" (Numbers 33:51-56.)

THE SEVEN ENEMIES

Let us next look in detail at the seven enemies of the Joshua Generation that we must overcome.

1. Materialism (Canaanites)

The Canaanites were merchant traders, known for their business skill and material possessions. The first enemy, materialism, is one of the greatest enemies of God in the earth today, especially in the western church that lives in a society that has an unquenchable lust for wealth and possessions. The spirit of covetousness will rob you from your promised land in God.

The nation Israel in the wilderness is a type of the Church of God. (Acts 7:38.) The Bible says that their clothes and shoes never wore out in the forty years they were in the wilderness. We see how God supernaturally fed and protected them. We also see how God gave them the wealth of the heathen when they left Egypt. The children of Israel took all the gold and silver out of Egypt. "Now the children of Israel had done according to the word of Moses, and they had asked from the Egyptians articles of silver, articles of gold, and clothing. And the LORD had given the people favor in the sight of the Egyptians, so that they granted them what they requested. Thus they plundered the Egyptians." (Exodus 12:35, 36.)

This is a picture of God's desire and ability to provide for His people. God doesn't delight in His people being poor and living in lack. He delights in the prosperity of His people!

According to Psalms 35:27, "Let them shout for joy and be glad, who favor my righteous cause; and let them say continually, 'Let the LORD be magnified, who has pleasure in the prosperity of His servant.'"

The Lord wants us to look to Him for all our needs, and to overcome the spirit of materialism. Jesus said, "No one can serve two masters; for either he will hate the one and love the other, or else he will be loyal to the one and despise the other. You cannot serve God and mammon." (Matthew 6:24.)

You cannot serve God and money both. Don't let your heart's desire be in money or possessions. Let it be in the true and living God. It is God's desire to care and provide for you, but He can't until you seek Him first and place His kingdom first in your life. "'Therefore do not worry, saying,

"What shall we eat?" or "What shall we drink?" or "What shall we wear?" For after all these things the Gentiles seek. For your heavenly Father knows that you need all these things. But seek first the kingdom of God and His righteousness, and all these things shall be added to you. Therefore do not worry about tomorrow, for tomorrow will worry about its own things. Sufficient for the day is its own trouble.'" (Matthew 6:31-34.)

Jesus said that if we seek first His kingdom, that everything needed shall be added unto us. God is not against us having things. He is against things having us! Remember: a kingdom vision produces kingdom provision!

We read in 1 Timothy 6:6-13: "Now godliness with contentment is great gain. For we brought nothing into this world, and it is certain we can carry nothing out. And having food and clothing, with these we shall be content. But those who desire to be rich fall into temptation and a snare, and into many foolish and harmful lusts which drown men in destruction and perdition. For the love of money is a root of all kinds of evil, for which some have strayed from the faith in their greediness, and pierced themselves through with many sorrows.

"But you, O man of God, flee these things and pursue righteousness, godliness, faith, love, patience, gentleness. Fight the good fight of faith, lay hold on eternal life, to which you were also called and have confessed the good confession in the presence of many witnesses."

Those that have set out to "get rich quick" have fallen into a snare of the enemy. That lifestyle will cause you to drown in stress and sorrow. However, it is not money that is evil, dear saint. It is the ruthless pursuit and love of money that is evil. Money can be a great blessing or a great curse in your life.

The Greek word "coveted" means "to stretch out one's self in order to grasp something." The picture this word gives me is of a little child reaching for the cookie jar that is just out of his reach. Materialism and the possessing of things will not satisfy the longing of your heart. Don't be seduced by the spirit of materialism and covetousness. That spirit will put you in debt, ruin your health and break up your home.

God wants to bless you with His blessing. He wants you to be a giver and to have a vision for helping to finance world evangelism. He wants you to live a contented life. He wants you to trust and believe Him to meet your every need. "And my God shall supply all your need according to His riches in glory by Christ Jesus." (Philippians 4:19)

2. Fear (Hittites)

The Hittite tribe was a fierce nation that brought terror and fear into the hearts of its enemies. The spirit of fear is an enemy of the Joshua Generation because fear has the power to literally destroy your life. The spirit of fear is not a benign, innocent little problem. Fear is an evil spirit from hell, and it will steal, kill, and destroy your life if you let it. Fear is the product of thinking on thoughts of failure. Fear is the "devil's faith." It causes things to come to pass the same way that faith does. For example, we read, "For the thing I greatly feared has come upon me, and what I dreaded has happened to me." (Job 3:25.)

Job literally said, "I feared a fear and it came to pass." Fear is an invitation for Satan to work in your life, just as faith is an open door for God to work. Proverbs 10:24 says, "The fear of the wicked will come upon him, and the desire of the righteous will be granted."

We can overcome the spirit of fear and drive it out of our lives by God's Word. "For God has not given us a spirit of fear, but of power and of love and of a sound mind." (2 Timothy 1:7.)

Fear is a spirit, but it is not from God. It will hurt you unless you conquer it in your life. The above verse gives us God's three keys to overcoming the spirit of fear in our lives.

The first key to overcoming fear is to receive a revelation of the power of God that is in us! God has given us His power! "But you shall receive power when the Holy Spirit has come upon you; and you shall be witnesses to Me in Jerusalem, and in all Judea and Samaria, and to the end of the earth." (Acts 1:8.) We have received the same power that raised Christ from the dead, and God wants you to know and believe in His power in you. Jesus said that He has given us "the authority to trample on serpents and scorpions, and over all the power of the enemy, and nothing shall by any means hurt" us. (Luke 10:19.)

Ephesians 6:10 tells us to "be strong in the Lord and in the power of His might." We have overcome by what Christ has already done, and He wants us to experience that victory on a personal level. "You are of God, little children, and have overcome them, because He who is in you is greater than he who is in the world." (1 John 4:4.)

The second key to overcoming fear is to receive a revelation of the love of God. Love is greater than fear, and as you receive and believe in God's love for you, fear will leave! 1 John 4:16, 18 says, "And we have known and believed the love that God has for us. God is love, and he who abides in love abides in God, and God in him...There is no fear in love; but perfect love casts out fear, because fear involves torment. But he who fears has not been made perfect in love." God's love drives fear out of your life!

Fear will ruin your health and shorten your life. God wants you to conquer fear by receiving and believing His great love for you. Romans 8:35-39 reads: "Who shall separate us from the love of Christ? Shall tribulation, or distress, or persecution, or famine, or nakedness, or peril, or sword? As it is written: 'For Your sake we are killed all day long; we are accounted as sheep for the slaughter.' Yet in all these things we are more than conquerors through Him who loved us. For I am persuaded that neither death nor life, nor angels nor principalities nor powers, nor things present nor things to come, nor height nor depth, nor any other created thing, shall be able to separate us from the love of God which is in Christ Jesus our Lord."

The third key to overcoming the spirit of fear is to receive a sound mind. The Greek word for "sound" means "discipline and self-control." God has given us a disciplined mind, a mind that can filter out the garbage of the world and the attacks of the devil. An undisciplined mind is incapable of maintaining victory, and it will keep you in a circle of failure and fear.

We have the mind of Christ as believers. "For 'who has known the mind of the LORD that he may instruct Him?' But we have the mind of Christ." (1 Corinthians 2:16.) You don't have to receive every thought Satan throws at you. God wants to make your mind sharp and active and filled with His Word. According to Paul, "though we walk in the flesh, we do not war according to the flesh. For the weapons of our warfare are not carnal but mighty in God for pulling down strongholds, casting down arguments and every high thing that exalts itself against the knowledge of God, bringing every thought into captivity to the obedience of Christ, and being ready to punish all disobedience when your obedience is fulfilled." (2 Corinthians 10:3-6.) Cast down wrong thoughts and attitudes. Bring all your thoughts into alignment with God's Word.

God has given you self-control as a part of the fruit of the Spirit. He has given you the mind of Christ. He has given you a disciplined mind. Use this wonderful gift of God to drive out fear!

God has called you to conquer the power of the spirit of fear. As the world continues to become an increasingly fearful place to live, guard your mind and heart from fear, and stay in God's Word by meditating day and night on His precious promises.

According to Isaiah 43:1-2, 5: "But now, thus says the LORD, who created you, O Jacob, and He who formed you, O Israel: 'Fear not, for I have redeemed you; I have called you by your name; you are Mine. When you pass through the waters, I will be with you; and through the rivers, they shall not overflow you. When you walk through the fire, you shall not be burned, nor shall the flame scorch you...Fear not, for I am with you.'"

And Isaiah 41:10 says, "'Fear not, for I am with you; be not dismayed, for I am your God. I will strengthen you, yes, I will help you, I will uphold you with My righteous right hand.'"

3. Humanism (Hivites)

The Hebrew definition of the Hivites is "to live a life, openly shown, a serpent." This tribe is a type of the spirit of humanism. This spirit is one of the strongest, if not the strongest, of all evil spirits at work today in the world. It is the exaltation of man to the place of God. Humanism and Christianity are opposites, and they will war against each other until Christ comes again.

The spirit of humanism is the reason for the fall of man: Adam and Eve's desire "to be like God." "Now the serpent was more cunning than any beast of the field which the LORD God had made. And he said to the woman, 'Has God indeed said, "You shall not eat of every tree of the garden"?' And the woman said to the serpent, 'We may eat the fruit of the trees of the garden; but of the fruit of the tree which is in the midst of the garden, God has said, "You shall not eat it, nor shall you touch it, lest you die."'"

"Then the serpent said to the woman, 'You will not surely die. For God knows that in the day you eat of it your eyes will be opened, and you will be like God, knowing good and evil.' So when the woman saw that the tree was good for food, that it was pleasant to the eyes, and a tree desirable to make one wise, she took of its fruit and ate. She also gave to her husband with her, and he ate. Then the eyes of both of them were opened, and they knew that they were naked; and they sewed fig leaves together and made themselves coverings." (Genesis 3:1-7.)

You can hear the sound of the serpent's hiss when Satan tells Eve, "And you shall be as gods, knowing good and evil." That is the lure of humanism -- to be a god. Here, Satan delights in deceiving God's creation into ignoring their Creator, and exalting themselves in their hearts and minds. The devil used this same approach to try and tempt Christ: "Then Peter took Him aside and began to rebuke Him, saying, 'Far be it from You, Lord; this shall not happen to You!' But He turned and said to Peter, 'Get behind Me, Satan! You are an offense to Me, for you are not mindful of the things of God, but the things of men.' Then Jesus said to His disciples, 'If anyone desires to come after Me, let him deny himself, and take up his cross, and follow Me. For whoever desires to save his life will lose it, but whoever loses his life for My sake will find it.'" (Matthew 16:22-25.)

Satan had filled Peter's heart with the spirit of humanism, and when Jesus told of His upcoming death, Peter answered and said, "Far be it from You, Lord." The Greek literally reads, "Think of or pity yourself." The cross of Christ was a death to His "self-life," and Satan tried to stop the cross by causing Christ to "pity Himself."

Satan will try and stop you from fully following God by tempting you to "think of yourself" or "pity yourself." But Christianity is a death of our "old man" so that we can live as "new creatures" in Christ Jesus. "I have been crucified with Christ; it is no longer I who live, but Christ lives in me; and the life which I now live in the flesh I live by faith in the Son of God, who loved me and gave Himself for me." (Galatians 2:20.)

Jesus went on to say in Matthew 16 that if any man would follow Him, He would have to deny his self-life. You can and must control your "old man," -- your Adamic nature. Your "fleshly nature" must be continually subdued and conquered by your new man.

Jesus told us to take up our cross and follow Him. Our cross is to follow God's path for our lives. As Christ prayed, "Not my will but Yours be done," we, too, must overcome our flesh and follow the path of Christ. Our cross means this:

Calvary's Road Of Self Sacrifice

4. Immorality (Perizzite)

The Hebrew word Perizzite means "open, unwalled." This

tribe was a roaming tribe that never bothered to secure its dwelling by building walls and cities. This open, unprotected existence is a type of what the spirit of immorality produces in people's lives. We live in a society that rejected God's Word concerning the sacredness and sanctity of sex, and because they have broken His law, they are reaping the consequences. There are more brokenhearted people in our society right now than any other time in history.

1 Corinthians 6:15-20 says: "Do you not know that your bodies are members of Christ? Shall I then take the members of Christ and make them members of a harlot? Certainly not! Or do you not know that he who is joined to a harlot is one body with her? For 'the two,' He says, 'shall become one flesh.' But he who is joined to the Lord is one spirit with Him.

"Flee sexual immorality. Every sin that a man does is outside the body, but he who commits sexual immorality sins against his own body.19 Or do you not know that your body is the temple of the Holy Spirit who is in you, whom you have from God, and you are not your own?20 For you were bought at a price; therefore glorify God in your body and in your spirit, which are God's."

When you have sexual relations with someone, you are spiritually joined to that person. You become "one flesh."

This union causes the walls of your soul to be battered down, and it opens your life up to demonic oppression. God has reserved sex for marriage alone. The plague of incurable and deadly sexually transmitted diseases is a physical manifestation of the spiritual destruction that immorality brings to a person's life. The Bible says that this sin is a "sin against your own body."

We read in Proverbs 6:26-29, 32-33: "For by means of a harlot a man is reduced to a crust of bread; and an adulteress will prey upon his precious life. Can a man take fire to his bosom, and his clothes not be burned? Can one walk on hot coals, and his feet not be seared? So is he who goes in to his neighbor's wife; whoever touches her shall not be innocent…Whoever commits adultery with a woman lacks understanding; he who does so destroys his own soul. Wounds and dishonor he will get, and his reproach will not be wiped away."

According to verse 32, he that commits adultery "destroys his own soul." This "soul destruction" is caused by our rejecting the instruction of God by defiling our bodies in sexual impurity.

There is a plague of immorality sweeping our nation, and it is also sweeping much of the Church. This sin will stop you from becoming what God has called you to be, and it will stop you from fulfilling all that God has called you to do. You can overcome the spirit of lust and the spirit of immorality. God can deliver you from past sexual relationships. God wants you to be an undefiled vessel that is sexually clean and pure.

Understand something very important, dear believer: GOD invented sex. It was His idea. He has given us the boundaries of marriage for sex to he enjoyed and practiced in. Satan has corrupted and counterfeited God's great idea. Sex will destroy you outside of marriage!

You cannot fill your mind with "R" rated and "X" rated movies, or pornographic magazines, and be "okay" with God. That filthy garbage will defile you and open your life to demonic influence. Remember this: garbage in, garbage out! Don't let your heart and eyes be filled with garbage and immoral materials. Flee those temptations, and live as a pure, powerful vessel for God.

5. Compromise (Girgashites)

The Girgashites were "dwellers of the clay or marsh." They speak to us of compromised living. They were a type of living in "gray areas." Satan couldn't stop you from being saved. He couldn't stop you from getting baptized in water and filled with the Spirit. In fact, he really isn't that upset about "losing you," unless you decide to live as an uncompromising Christian. Then, believe me, you will get his attention! Most of your friends and family members aren't real upset that you "got saved," as long as you don't become a "fanatic."

The greatest enemy to true revival in our land is compromising Christians and compromising Christianity. Jesus said, "'I know your works, that you are neither cold nor hot. I could wish you were cold or hot. So then, because you are lukewarm, and neither cold nor hot, I will vomit you out of My mouth.'" (Revelation 3:15, 16.)

We are to be hot and on fire for God! And yes, we may offend some people, especially "religious people," but it is better to offend people than to offend God! "But Peter and the other apostles answered and said: 'We ought to obey God rather than men.'" (Acts 5:29.)

Compromise produces confusion in the life of the believer. Compromise brings frustration in the life of the people of God, because you will eventually lose whatever you've compromised to keep. The pressure to "conform to the norm" must be countered by our bold witness and example. God is looking for champions!

The Joshua Generation is an uncompromising generation that refuses to settle for anything but God's best.

In Romans 12:2 we read: "And do not be conformed to

this world, but be transformed by the renewing of your mind, that you may prove what is that good and acceptable and perfect will of God." The Church should not look like, act like or think like the lost, dying world. We are to be light to the darkness around us. The darkness cannot put out the light. In Matthew 5:13-16 Jesus said: "'You are the salt of the earth; but if the salt loses its flavor, how shall it be seasoned? It is then good for nothing but to be thrown out and trampled underfoot by men. You are the light of the world. A city that is set on a hill cannot be hidden. Nor do they light a lamp and put it under a basket, but on a lamp stand, and it gives light to all who are in the house. Let your light so shine before men, that they may see your good works and glorify your Father in heaven.'"

King Saul's anointing as king was stripped from him because he was a compromising leader. The sin of compromise brought demonic oppression, and eventually death, into his life. God wants us to obey all of His Word, and to conquer compromise. Saul rebelled against God by only doing part of His commandment. This opens the door to demonic activity, and it brings the judgment of God.

Our witness (light) must be seen and heard. God hasn't called you to be a "secret saint" anymore. It is time to awaken, O army of God, and be all that God has called us to be! We are living in the time of the "arise and shine" of the Body of Christ. God has stirred up and strengthened us for the greatest decade of victory and witness the Church has ever seen!

"Arise, shine; for your light has come! And the glory of the LORD is risen upon you. For behold, the darkness shall cover the earth, and deep darkness the people; but the LORD will arise over you, and His glory will be seen upon you." (Isaiah 60:1, 2.)

6. Rebellion/Pride (Amorites)

The Hebrew meaning of the tribe Amorites is "proud, boasting, bitter rebels, mountaineers." This sixth enemy of the Joshua Generation is a type of the spirit of rebellion or pride. The Amorites made their home in the thin air of the mountains. They were a nation of "bitter rebels." The only thing that holds together a group of bitter rebels is their common ground of pride and rebellion.

The spirit of pride is what caused Lucifer to sin in his heart and try to exalt himself above God. God hates pride. James 4:6-10 says that "He gives more grace. Therefore He says: 'God resists the proud, but gives grace to the humble.' Therefore submit to God. Resist the devil and he will flee from you. Draw near to God and He will draw near to you. Cleanse your hands, you sinners; and purify your hearts, you double-minded. Lament and mourn and weep!

Let your laughter be turned to mourning and your joy to gloom. Humble yourselves in the sight of the Lord, and He will lift you up."

In these verses, the Holy Spirit is correcting an attitude problem in our lives. Our approach to God must be with a humble and meek spirit. The pride of life is not from God. "Do not love the world or the things in the world. If anyone loves the world, the love of the Father is not in him. For all that is in the world -- the lust of the flesh, the lust of the eyes, and the pride of life -- is not of the Father but is of the world. And the world is passing away, and the lust of it; but he who does the will of God abides forever." (1 John 2:15-17.)

By humbling ourselves before God, we can conquer the spirit of pride. According to 1 Peter 5:5-7: "Likewise you younger people, submit yourselves to your elders. Yes, all of you be submissive to one another, and be clothed with humility, for 'God resists the proud, but gives grace to the humble.' Therefore humble yourselves under the mighty hand of God, that He may exalt you in due time...."

God resists the proud. Pride "shuts you out" of God's presence and provision. Pride will bring a fall in your life. "Pride goes before destruction and a haughty spirit before a fall." (Proverbs 16:18.) "A man's pride will bring him low, but the humble in spirit will retain honor." (Proverbs

29:23.)

7. Discouragement/Condemnation (Jebusites)

The literal meaning of Jebusite is "trodden down." This is a picture of Satan's strategy to discourage and condemn God's people. There has been a great attack of discouragement and weariness against the Body of Christ in this time. Satan has sought to afflict God's people with "battle fatigue" to try and stop what he knows God is about to do.

Every Christian faces the battle against being discouraged and giving up. As God's people, God has given us a resilient spirit that refuses to let Satan keep us down. Micah7:7-8 tells us: "Therefore I will look to the LORD; I will wait for the God of my salvation; My God will hear me. Do not rejoice over me, my enemy; when I fall, I will arise; when I sit in darkness, the LORD will be a light to me; when I fall, I shall arise; when I sit in darkness, the Lord shall be a light unto me."

Satan is not only the Tempter and Deceiver; he is also the Accuser of the Church. God doesn't expect you never to fall. In fact, He knows you will. But God does expect you to get up after you've fallen. Satan is the one who tempts and deceives us into sin, and then he condemns us. The purpose of condemnation is to discourage us from going on in God. "For a righteous man may fall seven times and rise again, but the wicked shall fall by calamity." (Proverbs 24:16.)

A champion is not someone who has never, or will never, fall, but a champion of God is someone who refuses to stay down! Paul tells us that "there is therefore now no condemnation to those who are in Christ Jesus, who do not walk according to the flesh, but according to the Spirit. For the law of the Spirit of life in Christ Jesus has made me free from the law of sin and death." (Romans 8:1, 2.)

Resist and rebuke the condemner when he brings his discouraging voice around you. Don't let the mistakes of the past rob you from the victory for today and the future!

King David was out to war with his mighty men. When he came home, he found that his village was burned, and his family was taken hostage by the Amalekites. His first response was to cry for the loss he and his men had suffered. However, then he did something that enabled him not only to receive back all that was stolen, but also to plunder his enemy. "Now David was greatly distressed, for the people spoke of stoning him, because the soul of all the people was grieved, every man for his sons and his daughters. But David encouraged himself in the LORD his God." (1 Samuel 30:6.)

David encouraged himself in the Lord. The Hebrew word for "encourage" means "to seize, conquer, be strong, repair, bind." David conquered discouragement, and then all that was lost was restored back to him. Believer, if you can conquer discouragement, you can then retrieve what Satan stole.

Galatians 6:9 tells us to "not grow weary while doing good, for in due season we shall reap if we do not lose heart."

You shall reap if you don't quit! How many times have God's people given up the battle right before they would have reaped a tremendous victory? Satan can't win, unless he can so discourage you that you quit.

The Joshua Generation has the spirit of a champion! They refuse to stay down when they are knocked down. They refuse to let their hearts grow weary in well-doing. They press on for the prize of the high calling. They cannot be defeated!

CHAPTER 11:
RENEWING THE MIND

When the children of Israel had all crossed over the Jordan
River, they made camp in a place called Gilgal. This was their
base of operations for possessing the land.

Immediately after they had made camp at Gilgal, God
spoke to Joshua and told him to circumcise all the males of
Israel. "At that time the LORD said to Joshua, 'Make flint
knives for yourself, and circumcise the sons of Israel again
the second time.' So Joshua made flint knives for himself,
and circumcised the sons of Israel at the hill of the foreskins.
And this is the reason why Joshua circumcised them: All the
people who came out of Egypt who were males, all the men
of war, had died in the wilderness on the way, after they had
come out of Egypt. For all the people who came out had been
circumcised, but all the people born in the wilderness, on the
way as they came out of Egypt, had not been circumcised.

"So it was, when they had finished circumcising all the people that they stayed in their places in the camp till they were healed. Then the LORD said to Joshua, 'This day I have rolled away the reproach of Egypt from you.' Therefore the name of the place is called Gilgal to this day." (Joshua 5:2-5, 8, 9.)

Gilgal means "rolling away," and it was here at Gilgal that God "rolled away" the reproach of Egypt from His people. Circumcision is a perfect type of the believer renewing his mind with God's word!

The generation that died in the wilderness also had a physical circumcision, but God was not ultimately looking for an outward change. He was looking for a circumcision of their hearts He had brought them out of Egypt and now He wanted to take Egypt out of them. God has not only saved you from hell and the world, but He also wants to take the world out of you by renewing your mind.

Deuteronomy 10:16 says, "Therefore circumcise the foreskin of your heart, and be stiff-necked no longer." And Deuteronomy 30:5-6 says that "the LORD your God will bring you to the land which your fathers possessed and you shall possess it. He will prosper you and multiply you more than your fathers. And the LORD your God will circumcise your heart and the heart of your descendants, to love the LORD your God with all your heart and with all your soul that you may live."

When you were born again, your spirit came into perfect relationship with God. By the Blood of Jesus Christ, you were justified, sanctified and made perfectly righteous. Your name was written in the Lamb's Book of Life, and heaven became your home. You were given eternal life and delivered from hell. Your salvation experience is a one-time final and eternal decision. It is finished and completed. But is God done with you after you've been born again? Hardly! He's just begun with you.

Now that you are on your way to heaven (when you die or when Jesus comes again), God wants to bring heaven down to you! "And do not be conformed to this world, but be transformed by the renewing of your mind, that you may prove what is that good and acceptable and perfect will of God." (Romans 12:2.)

We are not to be conformed or patterned like this world. We shouldn't look like, live like or think like the world. God delivered Israel from Egypt, but He had a hard time taking Egypt out of the children of Israel. Don't conform to the world's system of living, but be transformed -- completely changed by the renewing of your mind with God's word. God's word will transform your life as you renew your mind with it.

**The Joshua Generation is a generation of believers
that has learned the secret of transformed living.**

RENOVATION

Just like with physical circumcision, the renewing of the
mind begins with a "cutting away of the flesh." The Greek
word for "renewing" means "to renovate." Renovation begins
by stripping off the old in order to put on the new. This
process is at the very center of the renovation of our minds.
God wants to strip away and tear down the wrong thinking
and believing that has been keeping you out of your
promised land. His Word will tear down those strongholds as
we confront the strongholds with the truth. "For though we
walk in the flesh, we do not war according to the flesh. For
the weapons of our warfare are not carnal but mighty in God
for pulling down strongholds, casting down arguments and
every high thing that exalts itself against the knowledge of
God, bringing every thought into captivity to the obedience
of Christ." (2 Corinthians 10:3-5.)

Dear saint, we are in a war. It is a battle between life and
death, good and evil, God and Satan. This battle is fought
on the battlefield of your mind. In these last days, Satan has
begun his greatest attack against the minds of men. We must
live in a military alertness against Satan's attack!

We are told to cast down imaginations (thoughts or

reasonings). This is how to do spiritual warfare for our souls: we must capture our thought life and bring it into obedience to God's Word. Until you learn to cast down and capture wrong, destructive thoughts and attitudes, it is impossible for you to live in victory as a believer.

God has a promised land for you, saint! It is a place of His provision and power. It is a place of kingdom life, love, joy and peace. This "promised land" is obtained by renewing your mind with His Word. This is God's system for victorious and successful living.

"Then Jesus said to those Jews who believed Him, 'If you abide in My word, you are My disciples indeed. And you shall know the truth, and the truth shall make you free.'" (John 8:31, 32) Jesus said that "the truth shall make you free." But understand this, even though the truth can make you free, there is a condition. Jesus gave this condition in verse 31 when He said, "If you abide in my word." Jesus emphasized that a disciple is one who continues in His Word. In order to know the truth and be set free, you must be a disciple who continues in God's Word.

You can't be a half-hearted or compromising Christian and expect to receive and know the truth that will set you free. God's Word requires a strong, consistent commitment in order to benefit from its potential power. God wants to write His Word in our minds. "For this is the covenant that

I will make with the house of Israel after those days, says the LORD: I will put My laws in their mind and write them on their hearts; and I will be their God, and they shall be My people." (Hebrews 8:10.) "This is the covenant that I will make with them after those days, says the LORD: 'I will put My laws into their hearts, and in their minds I will write them...'" (Hebrews 10:16.)

Jesus understood the vital importance of our souls being filled with God's Word. In Matthew 15:18, 19, He described the soul and how it functions: "'But those things which proceed out of the mouth come from the heart, and they defile a man. For out of the heart proceed evil thoughts, murders, adulteries, fornications, thefts, false witness, blasphemies." Jesus told us here that a man's life (what he does) is controlled by what is in his heart. The Paraphrased Version of Matthew 15:18 reads that "it is the thought life that pollutes."

Your soul is like the soil of a farm -- whatever is planted into it produces a crop. In the parable of the sower, Jesus taught about four different types of ground. These four types of ground are four types of heart conditions. In every different soil, the ground produces whatever was sown into it. In the same way, your soul (which is your mind, will and emotions) is designed to produce whatever is sown into it. "For as he thinks in his heart, so is he." (Proverbs 23:7.)

Your soul works scientifically, just like your body. If you eat junk food and never exercise, your body will suffer. Also, if you feed your soul garbage all the time, you will reap garbage. You are not a garbage dump for Satan and the world! You are a child of God, and God wants to fill you with the priceless treasure of His Word!

THE WORD OF GOD

Everything we will ever need as believers for our lives, God has given us in His Word. He has filled His Word with His life and power. "For the word of God is living and powerful, and sharper than any two-edged sword, piercing even to the division of soul and spirit, and of joints and marrow, and is a Discerner of the thoughts and intents of the heart." (Hebrews 4:12.)

God's Word pulsates with His power and life. God wants you to receive that life and power, and experience transformed living by renewing your mind. According to 2 Peter 1:2-4: "Grace and peace be multiplied to you in the knowledge of God and of Jesus our Lord, as His divine power has given to us all things that pertain to life and godliness, through the knowledge of Him who called us by glory and virtue, by which have been given to us exceedingly great and precious promises, that through these you may be partakers of the divine nature, having escaped the corruption that is in the world through lust."

God has given us all things we need through the knowledge of His Word. These precious promises enable us to become "partakers of the divine nature." This "divine nature" is having the mind of Christ. We receive the mind of Christ by receiving and believing His Word.

DISCIPLES OF THE WORD

In the fifth chapter of Joshua, we see that, right after their circumcision -- which is a type of renewing our minds, -- "the manna ceased on the day after they had eaten the produce of the land; and the children of Israel no longer had manna, but they ate the food of the land of Canaan that year." (Joshua 5:12.)

It is God's will for you to become a disciple of His Word. The manna the children of Israel received from God everyday is symbolic of Christians being fed the Word of God by their pastor and other five-fold ministers. It is good to receive "fresh manna" from anointed ministers, but just like a little baby who is growing up, God wants to teach you how to "live off the land" -- how to feed and grow in God's Word in your own study and daily reading.

The Joshua Generation isn't content to live off of Sunday's sermon for the whole week. They are studying every day for their "daily bread" of God's Word.

"Be diligent to present yourself approved to God, a worker who does not need to be ashamed, rightly dividing the word of truth." (2 Timothy 2:15.) Don't live off of someone else's revelation. Let God's Word become your soul's greatest hunger and quest. God's Word will work for you!

"All Scripture is given by inspiration of God, and is profitable for doctrine, for reproof, for correction, for instruction in righteousness, that the man of God may be complete, thoroughly equipped for every good work." (2 Timothy 3:16, 17.) God's Word will profit your life. It will transform your soul, and as your soul is changed, you will experience more and more of God's life and power.

God is love. He is our loving Heavenly Father, and He wants you to prosper and be in health. "Beloved, I pray that you may prosper in all things and be in health, just as your soul prospers." (3 John 1:2.) He wants to heal you and bring victory and success into your life. However, He can only prosper you as your soul prospers. As you receive God's Word, your soul will prosper. God's Word will transform your life as you renew your mind.

The healing, prospering and perfecting of your soul is a life-long process. That doesn't mean you are earning salvation. It simply means that your soul needs constant renewal and renovation as you constantly change into the image of Christ.

God's implanted Word is filled with His life and power to

save your soul. "Therefore lay aside all filthiness and overflow of wickedness, and receive with meekness the implanted word, which is able to save your souls." (James 1:21.) The salvation of your soul (mind, will and emotions) is not a one-time experience, but it is a daily journey for the rest of your life. As you plant the seeds of God's Word into the good soil of your heart, it will produce a crop of God's power and provision. Fill your mind with God's Word and experience the power of transformed living!

CHAPTER 12:
THE MOSES VS. JOSHUA GENERATION

For the first time in history, God has placed the desire to take cities for God in the hearts of tens of thousands of believers in the Body of Christ. There is a forceful and warring spirit in the Church today. It is not anger against men, but a holy anger against Satan's dominion and destruction in the earth.

Jesus said, "And from the days of John the Baptist until now the kingdom of heaven suffers violence, and the violent take it by force." (Matthew 11:12.) We are "taking by force" our cities for God in this decade. We are "taking by force" our families by fighting for them in prayer. Satan can not have our loved ones, dear saint. He also cannot have our cities unless we simply lay down and surrender them to him. But we're not dead! We are alive and filled with the power of God's Spirit!

THE MOSES GENERATION

God sorrowfully watched the "Moses Generation" choose

to give up their inheritance by not crossing over into their promised land. Unbelief and fear kept them from receiving God's perfect will, and literally robbed them of their inheritance. "So all the congregation lifted up their voices and cried, and the people wept that night. And all the children of Israel complained against Moses and Aaron, and the whole congregation said to them, 'If only we had died in the land of Egypt! Or if only we had died in this wilderness!'" (Numbers 14:1, 2) They murmured and complained against Moses and the leaders. They murmured against God. The entire "Moses Generation" died in the wilderness. Many preachers have told us that "God killed them," but that is not the truth. They destroyed themselves with their unbelief and fear.

The Lord spoke right after the entire nation (except the two spies, Joshua and Caleb) had raised their voices in unbelief to reject God's will. "'Say to them, "As I live," says the LORD, "just as you have spoken in My hearing, so I will do to you."'" (Numbers 14:28.)

The Israelites own confession was that of death and de-struction. God couldn't make them do what they refused to do. Instead, they reaped the consequences of rejecting God's Word.

A DIFFERENT SPIRIT

Joshua and Caleb had a different spirit than the rest of the children of Israel. They had a "conquering vision," and they believed God's Word. The Lord prophesied that there would arise a whole generation of Joshua and Caleb's -- the Joshua Generation. He saw that through these believers and over-comers, the whole earth would be filled with His glory. "'But as truly, as I live, all the earth shall be filled with the glory of the LORD.'" (Numbers 14:21.)

God is raising up a generation of champions: men and women whom He has filled with fire and desire to see revival come to their cities and nations. He is raising up a generation that will be like Caleb, a generation that has a "different spirit" in them and who follow Him fully. (Numbers 14:24)

God wants you to be a part of the Joshua Generation. He wants to give you a spirit of boldness and authority so that you will rise up and be a HERO in these last days for him. Don't let this cloud and fire pass you by! Surrender to God and He will make you hero.

CHAPTER 13:
SENT TO THE CITIES

God is not calling Christians to abandon the cities of this nation and other nations. He is calling us take the cities. Why? For the obvious reason that they are filled with people. God loves people. He sent His Son to die for people. People are the most valuable treasure in all creation. They are of the greatest value in God's eyes.

Joshua went to look at the city of Jericho. "And it came to pass, when Joshua was by Jericho, that he lifted his eyes and looked." (Joshua 5:13.) We need to take another look at the city to where God has sent us. Why did God bring you to your city? To punish you or test you? No! He sent you as part of the answer for the deliverance of that city.

Jesus said, "'You are the salt of the earth; but if the salt loses its flavor, how shall it be seasoned? It is then good for nothing but to be thrown out and trampled underfoot by men. You are the light of the world. A city that is set on a hill cannot be hidden. Nor do they light a lamp and put it under a basket, but on a lampstand, and it gives light to all who are in the house. Let your light so shine before men, that they may see your good works and glorify your Father in heaven.'" (Matthew 5:13-16.)

God is raising up, in every city of the world, a light of salvation. There is to be "a city within the city." That "city" will be on a hill, and it will be a light to all of the rest of the city. God has sent us to the city in which we live for a divine purpose. That divine purpose is to be light and salt. In these last days, God is raising up an army of "city-takers" who no longer live on the defensive, but who are praying, preparing, making and implementing strategies to take their city for God! This "possessing spirit" is sweeping over the Body of Christ in these days.

Psalm 2:8 tells about this possessing spirit to take our cities for God: "'Ask of me, and I will give you the nations for your inheritance, and the ends of the earth for your possession." We are to ask God for our cities, and then begin to possess them by faith. The word "possession" here means "something seized by force." Is God capable of bringing revival to your city? Yes! Are you capable of believing God to do that? Yes! Then let us take our cities for God and see revival come to our land.

A church in a city that has no divine purpose will not only NOT affect its city, but it will produce defeated Christians who are seeking to survive the wickedness of their city rather than seeking to conquer it. Christianity is made for conquering and overcoming, not retreating. In Matthew 16:18, Jesus said that "the gates of hell" would not stop the army of God.

The end-time church will be filled with a divine purpose in regards to their cities. As you look at your city, what do you see? Can you see the possibility and potential of thousands coming into the Kingdom of God in your city? Why has God led you to the particular neighborhood in which you live? Instead of seeing yourself surrounded by a host of darkness trying to extinguish your light, can you see that God has sent you into the darkness of your city to bring the light of God's love and life?

"Arise, shine; for your light has come! And the glory of the LORD is risen upon you. For behold, the darkness shall cover the earth, and deep darkness the people; but the LORD will arise over you, and His glory will be seen upon you." (Isaiah 60:1, 2.) It is the hour of the "arise and shine" of the church. As you and I begin to show forth the life of God, the darkness is defeated by the light.

If your church and pastor has no "divine purpose" for your city, then begin to pray for God to give your pastor a vision for your city. If you are not a part of an on-fire church and don't have a Godly pastor, then immediately ask God to lead you to one. Find a church, and be committed and submitted. Help take your city for God. Find your place of ministry in a local body, and work together with that church to help win your city for God.

Jericho means "fragrant or sweet." To Joshua, the city was a "sweet place" of God's promises and provision. Your city may be overrun by pollution, crime, divorce and drugs. It may seem to be place of hopelessness and despair. But God wants to change what you see when you look at your city.

God loves your city. He loves the people in it. As you begin to pray for your city, it will become a "sweet place" for you. You will fall in love with it because God loves it. Then allow God's love to be a river of life flowing to the barren desert of a hurting humanity. Don't give up on your city and nation. God hasn't.

CHAPTER 14:
THE ANGEL OF THE CITY

As Joshua looked towards Jericho, he was startled to see another soldier standing before the city with his sword drawn in his hand. He was also looking at the City of Jericho because God had sent him there to help Joshua take the city.

God has sent a warring angel to every city of the world to help the church there take their city. This angel is a captain of a host of angels. He has been sent there by God. "And it came to pass, when Joshua was by Jericho, that he lifted his eyes and looked, and behold, a Man stood opposite him with His sword drawn in His hand. And Joshua went to Him and said to Him, "Are You for us or for our adversaries?'" (Joshua 5:13.)

In these last days, there is going to be a tremendous increase in angelic activity in the world. Angels are instruments of God's will. In Hebrews 1:14, the Bible tells us they are to serve believers: "Are they not all ministering spirits sent forth to minister for those who will inherit salvation?" Angels are assigned to protect and deliver God's people. "The angel of the LORD encamps all around those who fear Him, and delivers them." (Psalm 34:7.) And "For He shall give His angels charge over you, to keep you in all your ways. In their hands they shall bear you up, lest you dash your foot against a stone." (Psalm 91:11, 12.)

Angels respond exclusively to God's Word. When we are acting on and obeying and believing God's Word, then we may have angelic help. Psalm 103:20 tells us: "Bless the LORD, you His angels, who excel in strength, who do His word, heeding the voice of His word."

When we find God's divine purpose, we also tap into His power and provision to accomplish His purpose. It is God's purpose to win your city. When His divine purpose becomes our purpose, we see His unlimited power and purpose flow into our lives.

Exodus 23:20-23 tells us more about the angel of our city: "'Behold, I send an Angel before you to keep you in the way and to bring you into the place which I have prepared. Beware of Him and obey His voice; do not provoke Him, for He will not pardon your transgressions; for My name is in Him. But if you indeed obey His voice and do all that I speak, then I will be an enemy to your enemies and an adversary to your adversaries. For My Angel will go before you and bring you in to the Amorites and the Hittites and the Perizzites and the Canaanites and the Hivites and the Jebusites; and I will cut them off.'"

I believe we can boldly and confidently send out angels to accomplish God's will. They respond to God's Word and will. It is God's will to take your city. Every week during our prayer time, we send out angels to bring in the harvest of souls. We also pray for angels to bring in God's provision for our church and our ministries.

I believe that when we go to heaven (either when Jesus comes back or when we die), you will meet the angel assigned to help you take our city. Many ministers and churches will look and see this gigantic warrior and his army that was assigned to work for them, and they will suddenly realize that they could have taken their city. I can picture this warrior of God walking up to a pastor and saying, "I am a warrior for God. I was assigned the city you lived and pastored in for years. I waited for you to assign me to work. Why didn't you release me to accomplish God's will?"

CHAPTER 15:
GOD'S DIVINE PURPOSE

Joshua was totally confident that it was God's will to take Jericho. He asked the angel of God if he was going to help him take the city: "Are you for us or against us?" The angel answered back with a surprising answer: "Neither." In these last days, God is no longer going to bless our attempts to accomplish His will. God's will must be done God's way! Our programs and plans will no longer be sufficient to accomplish God's will. We have used cute, creative programs instead of seeking and releasing God's power to our city.

We read in Joshua 5:13, 14: "And it came to pass, when Joshua was by Jericho, that he lifted his eyes and looked, and behold, a Man stood opposite him with His sword drawn in His hand. And Joshua went to Him and said to Him, 'Are You for us or for our adversaries?' So He said, 'No, but as Commander of the army of the LORD I have now come.'"

Verse 14 goes on to tells us that Joshua "fell down on his face and began to worship." God's purposes are found in His presence. We must fall on our faces before the throne of God and seek God's will and way. In worship, there is a manifestation of humility. If we attempt to do the right or good thing for God, and yet do not seek Him first for direction and guidance, then we are acting out of pride and our own ability and sufficiency.

Numbers 14:44, 45 tells us that "they presumed to go up to the mountaintop. Nevertheless, neither the ark of the covenant of the LORD nor Moses departed from the camp. Then the Amalekites and the Canaanites who dwelt in that mountain came down and attacked them, and drove them back as far as Hormah."

Presumption is when we do the right thing the wrong way. Without God's divine purpose and His revealed will, we will fail. Joshua was worshipping the Lord on his face when he said, "What does My LORD say to his servant?" At the feet of our Lord and Savior, we receive His divine purpose. In God's plan is God's power and provision.

The Joshua Generation is believers who have laid down their own will and plans in order to receive God's plans and purposes. Our cry must be, "What does my Lord say to His servant?"

God wants to reveal His purpose to us. "'Call to Me, and I will answer you, and show you great and mighty things, which you do not know.'" (Jeremiah 33:3.)

God has a divine purpose for your life. He has one for your church and your city. His purposes are found in the place of prayer and worship. The purposes of God destroy the purposes of hell. Let us seek the Lord until He speaks to us His divine purposes.

STRIPPING OFF OUR PLANS

In Joshua 5:15 we read the angel's answer as Joshua asked for God's purposes: "Then the Commander of the Lord's army said to Joshua, 'Take your sandal off your foot, for the place where you stand is holy.' And Joshua did so."

God's purposes begin by a "stripping off" of our own pursuits and plans. Joshua's shoes were symbolic of man's plans and man's ways. In the presence of God, our plans are stripped away. Joshua's shoes were taken off because the place was holy.

In the holy presence of God, we must remove what separates us from Him. Before we experience the power of God, we must experience the purity of God. Purity precedes God's power. In this last great move of God in the earth, God's power is not going to be guided and controlled by men. Instead, we are going to be guided and controlled by it. We are going to have a revival of God's glory and God's presence. God is going to be at the center of this world-shaking revival. No man, or man's plan, is going to overshadow God's presence and power.

Before God gives us cities and nations, He purifies the motives of our hearts. As we allow God to work in us, He then can work through us. God is raising up men and women of character in our time. His purposes will not be stopped by our weakness or our undeveloped character. That is why there is a tremendous cleansing going on right now in the ministry.

And not only is this cleansing going on the ministry, but it is also going on in the entire Body of Christ. He is purifying us to prepare us for His power and purpose. "For the time has come for judgment to begin at the house of God; and if it begins with us first, what will be the end of those who do not obey the Gospel of God?" (1 Peter 4:17.)

In the past moves of God, many times God's power was limited, or even lost, by a lack of character and purity in the ministry. That will not happen in God's next great move. Hebrews 12:1-3 tells us: "Therefore we also, since we are surrounded by so great a cloud of witnesses, let us lay aside every weight, and the sin which so easily ensnares us, and let us run with endurance the race that is set before us, looking unto Jesus, the author and finisher of our faith, who for the joy that was set before Him endured the cross, despising the shame, and has sat down at the right hand of the throne of God.

"For consider Him who endured such hostility from sinners against Himself, lest you become weary and discouraged in your souls"

God wants you to know His divine purpose for your life. God wants you to be a man or woman filled with divine purpose. We are living in the greatest hour the church has ever known. Don't let this day pass you by. As you seek the Lord and submit your life to Him, He will meet you and speak to you, give you life, Godly purpose and power, for our greatest hour.

CHAPTER 16:
THE ROAR OF GOD

God spoke to Joshua and told him, "I have given to your hand Jericho." This was a confirming and establishing word to Joshua. God wants to give us the cities of the world. If you are a pastor, God wants to give you a vision for taking your city. Without that vision, you will be spinning your wheels as a minister. You are either called to take a city for God or to work with someone who is.

We read in Joshua 6:1-5: "Now Jericho was securely shut up because of the children of Israel; none went out, and none came in. And the LORD said to Joshua: 'See! I have given Jericho into your hand, its king, and the mighty men of valor. You shall march around the city, all you men of war; you shall go all around the city once. This you shall do six days. And seven priests shall bear seven trumpets of rams' horns before the ark. But the seventh day you shall march around the city seven times, and the priests shall blow the trumpets. It shall come to pass, when they make a long blast with the ram's horn, and when you hear the sound of the trumpet, that all the people shall shout with a great shout; then the wall of the city will fall down flat. And the people shall go up every man straight before him.'"

The Lord then told Joshua to surround the city and march around it. This marching around the city is a picture of the army of God surrounding its city with prayer. There is a revival of prayer sweeping the earth right now. In this prayer revival, we are beginning to march around our cities. We are surrounding our cities with God's power. The children of Israel marched around the city one time a day for six days. God told them to march around the city seven times on the seventh day. I believe that God is calling us to not only pray, but to also pray without ceasing. When we increase our praying, we increase God's power in our lives and cities. Prayer produces power, and unceasing prayer produces unceasing power.

2 Chronicles 7:14-16 tells us "…if My people who are called by My name will humble themselves, and pray and seek My face, and turn from their wicked ways, then I will hear from heaven, and will forgive their sin and heal their land. Now My eyes will be open and My ears attentive to prayer made in this place."

Stop waiting for God to move! Start praying and watch God move!

We read in Joshua 6:16,20: "And the seventh time it happened, when the priests blew the trumpets, that Joshua said to the people: 'Shout, for the LORD has given you the city!'... So the people shouted when the priests blew the trumpets. And it happened when the people heard the sound of the trumpet, and the people shouted with a great shout, that the wall fell down flat. Then the people went up into the city, every man straight before him, and they took the city."

After they had marched around the city for seven days, the Lord told them to have the priest blow the trumpet and have the people shout. This sound of the trumpet and the shout of the people was the roar of God.

In every move of God, there is a sound that becomes the symbol of that move. It is a sound that is a part of what God is doing and saying. For example, during the late sixties and the seventies, the sound in the Charismatic Movement was a beautiful harmony of worship. Charismatic services had a "sweet sound" of the blending of God's people in a symphony of worship.

During this next move of God, the sound is going to be different. It will be a roar and a shout. God is putting a shout of victory into His people all over the earth. This shout is God roaring through His Body. It is the Lion of Judah declaring

His strength and might. As time comes to an end, and as we enter into a new millennium, God is winding this all up with a roar and a shout, not with a whisper and a whimper.

Joel 3:16 tells us that "the LORD also will roar from Zion, and utter His voice from Jerusalem; the heavens and earth will shake; but the LORD will be a shelter for His people, and the strength of the children of Israel." Zion is a type of the Church. And all over this country, and all over the world, there is a "new sound" being heard in the Church. It is a sound of war! It is a sound of joy! It is a shout of triumph!

Amos 1:2 says that "the LORD roars from Zion, and utters His voice from Jerusalem; the pastures of the shepherds mourn, and the top of Carmel withers." Out of Zion shall come a roar. When the children of Israel gave a shout and a roar, the walls came down. The walls are coming down in our lives, families and cities because God has begun to roar.

Hosea 11:10 tells us that "they shall walk after the LORD. He will roar like a lion. When He roars, then His sons shall come trembling from the west...." And Jeremiah 25:30 says: "Therefore prophesy against them all these words, and say to them: 'The LORD will roar from on high, and utter His voice from His holy habitation; He will roar mightily against His fold. He will give a shout, as those who tread the grapes, against all the inhabitants of the earth."

You can sense and feel the roar of God growing in the

Church. It is the voice of victory. It is the shout of war. It is the Spirit of God lifting a cry of victory in our midst. We read in Isaiah 42:13-14 that "the LORD shall go forth like a mighty man; He shall stir up His zeal like a man of war. He shall cry out, yes, shout aloud; He shall prevail against His enemies. 'I have held My peace a long time, I have been still and restrained Myself. Now I will cry like a woman in labor, I will pant and gasp at once.'"

We can see how the ROAR of God has brought down the Iron Curtain and the Berlin Wall. The Lord is beginning to roar out of Zion (the Church), and the earth shall hear His voice. He is warring against His enemies, and He has commissioned the Church to carry out His battle plans.

BORN IN A ROAR

In the New Testament, we see that the early Church was born in a roar.. There were 120 of the disciples of Jesus in Jerusalem, praying without ceasing. "When the Day of Pentecost had fully come, they were all with one accord in one place. And suddenly there came a sound from heaven, as of a rushing mighty wind, and it filled the whole house where they were sitting. Then there appeared to them divided tongues, as of fire, and one sat upon each of them. And they were all filled with the Holy Spirit and began to speak with other tongues, as the Spirit gave them utterance."

(Acts 2:1-4.)

Remember:

PRAYER PRODUCES POWER, AND UNCEASING PRAYER PRODUCES UNCEASING POWER!

Acts 2:2 tells us "how" God moved. God is moving, and it is surprising people how fast and how unexpectedly it is happening. "Suddenly there came a sound from heaven." This Greek word for sound is "echoes," which means "a loud noise; a roar." Suddenly there came a roar from heaven.

The roar of God birthed the Church. It was the roar of revival. The Church was birthed with a roar, and it will finish with even a greater roar. The greatest move of God the earth has ever known is before us right now!

Haggai 2:6-9 tells us more about the roar of the Lord: "For thus says the LORD of hosts: 'Once more (it is a little while) I will shake heaven and earth, the sea and dry land; and I will shake all nations, and they shall come to the Desire of All Nations, and I will fill this temple with glory,' says the LORD of hosts. 'The silver is Mine, and the gold is Mine,' says the LORD of hosts. 'The glory of this latter temple shall be greater than the former,' says the LORD of hosts. 'And in this place I will give peace,' says the LORD of hosts."

This next roar of God will come to the church and then from the church. It will sweep into every nation and people, every ethnic group and language. God's roar will be heard. His Spirit will flow into every nation. Can you hear it? I can! It is the roar of God!

CHAPTER 17
PROPHETIC PRAISE

There is a sound arising from the church in the earth today. It is a sound of rejoicing and victory, a sound of worship, a sound of war. God has unleashed a wave of militant and prophetic praise that is filling the church and cities of our world. The Holy Spirit has birthed a tremendous revival of praise and worship in these last days. New, anointed songs and choruses with a prophetic and triumphing theme are emerging from this "new sound" in the church.

We read in Psalm 149:1, 6-9: "Praise the LORD! Sing to the LORD a new song, and His praise in the assembly of saints...Let the high praises of God be in their mouth, and a two-edged sword in their hand, to execute vengeance on the nations, and punishments on the peoples; to bind their kings with chains, and their nobles with fetters of iron; to execute on them the written judgment - this honor have all His saints."

Through "High Praises," the church has entered into a new dimension and demonstration of spiritual warfare. Understanding that our praise and worship to God not only pleases and ministers to Him but they also destroy the works of hell around us! In this place of "High Praises," we prophetically proclaim God's purposes to our life, family, city, nation and world. The "sound of war" is being heard in the church.

We read in 2 Chronicles 20:1 "that the people of Moab with the people of Ammon, and others with them besides the Ammonites, came to battle against Jehoshaphat." The children of Israel were surrounded by their enemies. Adversity and opposition will happen to all men and especially to those who love and serve God, for when you decided to follow Christ, you became an enemy of the forces of hell in the earth. But God's plan is that you see His deliverance and salvation in the midst of your trouble.

After the king and nation began to seek God, they found his divine purpose for their lives. "And he said, 'Listen, all you of Judah and you inhabitants of Jerusalem, and you, King Jehoshaphat! Thus says the LORD to you: "Do not be afraid nor dismayed because of this great multitude, for the battle is not yours, but God's. You will not need to fight in this battle. Position yourselves, stand still and see the salvation of the

LORD, who is with you, O Judah and Jerusalem!"...Do not fear or be dismayed; tomorrow go out against them, for the LORD is with you.'" (2 Chronicles 20:15, 17.) God spoke to them and God will speak to you as you seek Him. The LORD has a "battle plan" for your life and His plan releases His Power.

In 2 Chronicles 20:21-22, we read, "And when he had consulted with the people, he appointed those who should sing to the LORD, and who should praise the beauty of holiness, as they went out before the army and were saying: 'Praise the LORD, For His mercy endures forever.' Now when they began to sing and to praise, the LORD set ambushes against the people of Ammon, Moab, and Mount Seir, who had come against Judah; and they were defeated."

When God's people began to sing His praise, it brought confusion to the enemies' camp. As we worship God together, Satan's army is brought into confusion and driven away. This next great move of God is going to be centered around the very presence of God in our midst. The lights of men's names and influence will dim and the light of God's glorious presence will shine brighter and brighter.

I believe that there is coming a creative anointing of new music and new songs that the earth has never heard before. Like a beautiful river of crystal clear water coming from the throne of God, this music will be the music of heaven in the earth. I believe that in the next years, the Spirit of Worship will be so strong in the church that it will be common place to sing and praise God for hours at a time.

God is going to bring His fullness to the church. This glory and presence of God will bring great miracles, healings, salvations and deliverance to all that are there. Out of this shall arise miraculous music that is literally filled with God's presence and power as we see happened in 2 Chronicles 5:13-14 when "it came to pass, when the trumpeters and singers were as one, to make one sound to be heard in praising and thanking the LORD, and when they lifted up their voice with the trumpets and cymbals and instruments of music, and praised the LORD, saying: 'For He is good, for His mercy endures forever,' that the house, the house of the LORD, was filled with a cloud, so that the priests could not continue ministering because of the cloud; for the glory of the LORD filled the house of God."

It is time for music to stop being for the purpose of entertaining the church. We must find and follow this stream of anointed, prophetic worship and let it carry us into the presence and purposes of God.

I have a vision inside of me of thousands and thousands of believers in every city in the world coming together to praise and worship God together. Spiritual warfare is released when we praise and worship God. When we come together to meet as the Church of the Living God, there should be an explosion of power and miracles in our midst.

This explosion of prophetic and victorious praise is the roar of God in the earth.

In 2 Chronicles 13:13-15, we see that God's people were surrounded. "But Jeroboam caused an ambush to go around behind them; so they were in front of Judah, and the ambush was behind them. And when Judah looked around, to their surprise the battle line was at both front and rear; and they cried out to the LORD, and the priests sounded the trumpets. Then the men of Judah gave a shout; and as the men of Judah shouted, it happened that God struck Jeroboam and all Israel before Abijah and Judah."

Judah means "celebration and praise." When Judah (who is a type of the church) shouted, God smote their enemy Jeroboam, whose name means "the people will contend." The strife and oppression of the world and Satan will be broken off you as you learn to shout and roar to and for God in the earth.

There is a new song in the land. Can you hear it? It is a song of deliverance being sung by the people of God in the earth.

CHAPTER 18:
PROSPERITY IN PERSPECTIVE

Is it God's will to prosper His children? That is the raging debate in the Body of Christ today. This war over prosperity has caused great confusion and conflict. However, prosperity takes on a whole new understanding when you uncover God's divine purpose for your life.

Yes, it is God's will to prosper you and meet your needs. As we read in Exodus 12:35-36: "Now the children of Israel had done according to the word of Moses, and they had asked from the Egyptians articles of silver, articles of gold, and clothing. And the LORD had given the people favor in the sight of the Egyptians, so that they granted them what they requested. Thus they plundered the Egyptians."

But the ultimate purpose for prosperity is not just to meet your needs. It is also for God to use you to meet the needs of others!

This understanding of the purpose and reason for prosperity is at the very core of God's provision in our life. The father of faith, Abraham, was birthed in this understanding of God's blessing. "I will make you a great nation; I will bless you and make your name great; and you shall be a blessing." (Genesis 12:2.l)

The Lord told him that he would "bless" and then "make him a blessing." God will bless you if you have a vision to be a blessing. This is the center of the purpose for prosperity. God's great end-time revival will be financed by believers who become channels of God's resources into the Kingdom of God. As we see exhibited in Joshua 6:24, God is looking for believers who will do as the Israelites did. When they had defeated Jericho, they didn't keep the spoils for themselves. Instead they took the "the silver and gold, and the vessels of bronze and iron" and put them "into the treasury of the house of the LORD." As you develop a vision for building the Kingdom of God, you then become a candidate for God's provision to flow through.

Jesus said in Matthew 6:33 that we should "seek first the kingdom of God and His righteousness, and all these things" would be added to us. **A KINGDOM VISION PRODUCES KINGDOM PROVISION.** The world seeks to get wealth and then horde it. God's people seek God's provision and prosperity to help others and build the Kingdom of God.

THE POWER TO GET WEALTH

Deuteronomy 8:18 tells us: "'And you shall remember the LORD your God, for it is He who gives you power to get wealth, that He may establish His covenant which He swore to your fathers, as it is this day.'"

The Lord spoke to me concerning this next move of God. He told me that we would not lack the resources necessary to accomplish His will. God will finance this next revival by giving His people "the power to get wealth." When you lose the purpose for prosperity, you lose the source of prosperity. As you build the kingdom of God, the kingdom of God will build you. Learn to give, and you'll have to give!

The greatest blessing of giving in God's Kingdom is that, first of all, giving conquers greed in our life. Secondly, giving is also God's pathway to receiving. The way you give is the way you'll live. When you've learned to give, you've learned to live!

According to Galatians 6:6-10, we should not "be deceived, God is not mocked; for whatever a man sows, that he will also reap. For he who sows to his flesh will of the flesh reap corruption, but he who sows to the Spirit will of the Spirit reap everlasting life. And let us not grow weary while doing good, for in due season we shall reap if we do not lose heart. Therefore, as we have opportunity, let us do good to all, especially to those who are of the household of faith."

We read in 2 Corinthians 9:6-9 that "He who sows sparingly will also reap sparingly, and he who sows bountifully will also reap bountifully. So let each one give as he purposes in his heart, not grudgingly or of necessity; for God loves a cheerful giver. And God is able to make all grace abound toward you, that you, always having all sufficiency in all things, may have an abundance for every good work."

If you aren't a tither, then you are a God-robber. And God-robbers are under the curse. If you tithe, but don't give offerings, then you are literally strangling the ability of God to bring abundance into your life. Tithing opens the windows of heaven, but offerings determine the size of blessing that will come to us.

"'Will a man rob God? Yet you have robbed Me! But you say, "In what way have we robbed You?" In tithes and offerings. You are cursed with a curse, for you have robbed Me, even this whole nation. Bring all the tithes into the storehouse, that there may be food in My house, and try Me now in this,' says the LORD of hosts, 'If I will not open for you the windows of heaven and pour out for you such blessing that there will not be room enough to receive it. And I will rebuke the devourer for your sakes, so that he will not destroy the fruit of your ground, nor shall the vine fail to bear fruit for you in the field,' says the LORD of hosts. 'And all nations will call you blessed, for you will be a delightful land,' says the

LORD of hosts." (Malachi 3:8-12.)

When people have trouble giving and tithing, it is not a money problem. It is a heart problem! Your giving determines the true feelings of your heart. Because we have "freely received," we are "freely to give." The greatest joy in life is to be a giver. God is a giver. He has given us His very best. As His children, let us never miss a chance to give. If we never miss an opportunity to give, in the abundant provision of God we will live!

CHAPTER 19
WARRING AGAINST THE GATES OF HELL

Joshua 10:17-19 tells us: "And it was told Joshua, saying, 'The five kings have been found hidden in the cave at Makkedah.' So Joshua said, 'Roll large stones against the mouth of the cave, and set men by it to guard them.'"

The five kings listed here in Joshua speak of the five different levels of satanic government and authority in the earth. Just as there is a "chain of command" in God's Kingdom, there also is a "chain of command" in Satan's kingdom. Understanding these five different levels of demonic authority is important to us in order to determine the strategy to defeat them.

For example, it is different to war against the spirit over a city than to war against the spirit over a person. There are different kinds of demonic forces at work. We see these five levels in Ephesians 6:10-12: "Finally, my brethren, be strong in the Lord and in the power of His might. Put on the whole armor of God, that you may be able to stand against the Wiles of the devil. For we do not wrestle against flesh and blood, but against principalities, against powers, against the rulers of the darkness of this age, against spiritual hosts of wickedness in the heavenly places."

Satan's government in the earth consists of:

1. **Principalities** - the "buck private;" the lowest level of Satan's command.
2. **Powers** - just above principalities in authority.
3. **Demons** (or **Evil Spirits**) - middle ranking; infantry level; foot soldiers.
4. **Spiritual Wickedness in High Places** - literally "evil spirits in the heavenlies;" upper management level spirits, like colonels or captains.
5. **Rulers of the Darkness of This World** - literally "world rulers;" spirits over nations and continents; Satan's generals.

Jesus said that "the gates of hell shall not prevail against it (the church)." What are the gates of hell? The gate in the Bible speaks of the place of authority and government. Jesus was saying that the government and authority of hell would not prevail against the church.

In Joshua 10:17, we see that the five kings were found hid in a cave at Makkedah. Makkedah means "place of the flocks; place of the shepherds." It is a picture of the local church. It is in the government and covering of a local church that God will reveal the government of Satan over cities and people. As we seek the Lord concerning our families and cities, the Lord will uncover and expose Satan's government to us.

When people get involved in spiritual warfare without the protection and covering of a local church, they will always get into some kind of trouble. They either become professional "demon chasers," or else they get wiped out in battle. I've seen believers who suddenly knew more than their pastor and other spiritual leaders, and who inwardly get into deception of some type. It seems Satan would either like the church to completely ignore him or be completely obsessed with him. God has called us to neither of these extremes, but to a balance of belief and practice.

Joshua put giant rocks at the mouth of the cave in which these five kings were hidden. He also assigned men to guard the cave. This is a picture of our authority as believers over Satan's forces. We read in Luke 10:17, 19 that when, "the seventy returned with joy, saying, 'Lord, even the demons are subject to us in Your name.'" Jesus then said to them, "'I saw Satan fall like lightning from heaven. Behold, I give you the authority to trample on serpents and scorpions , and over all the power of the enemy, and nothing shall by any means hurt you.'"

Jesus told us we had authority over all the power (strength and ability) of the government of Satan. We have authority over Satan himself and every one of his evil servants. It is time for the church to arise and take her place of authority so that God's Kingdom and purpose may be established in the earth.

God could have completely destroyed the seven nations of Canaan. He could have just vaporized them like He did Sodom and Gomorrah. Instead He left them there for God's people to conquer through Him.

Why, dear saint, has God allowed Satan to continue to exist? Why has He allowed this planet to be polluted by the wickedness of Satan's evil army? Why? Because God is going to display His strength and glory through the church to these evil powers. "To the intent that now the manifold wisdom of God might be made known by the church to the principalities and powers in the heavenly places." (Ephesians 3:10.)

God knows He can destroy Satan. However, His ultimate plan, His great masterpiece of glory, is for His people, the Church of Jesus Christ, to accomplish His will in the earth by destroying the works of hell. God has left us "giants in the land" because He has confidence that the Joshua Generation will defeat all His enemies.

Judges 3:1-3 tells us: "Now these are the nations which the LORD left, that He might test Israel by them, that is, all who had not known any of the wars in Canaan (this was only so that the generations of the children of Israel might be taught to know war, at least those who had not formerly known it), namely, five lords of the Philistines, all the Canaanites, the Sidonians, and the Hivites who dwelt in Mount Lebanon, from Mount Baal Hermon to the entrance of Hamath." The "five lords of the Philistines" spoken of here are also a picture of Satan's five levels of authority in the earth.

Spiritual warfare is not an option for the church. It is an absolute necessity if we want to live a victorious life in the Kingdom of God. Many ministers across our country have done a great injustice to God's people by ignoring, and even opposing, spiritual warfare. Teachings like this cripple the effectiveness and the ability of the church. We must be aware and awakened to the battle that is raging in the earth.

The Apostle Peter tells us to "be sober, be vigilant; because your adversary the devil walks about like a roaring lion, seeking whom he may devour." (1 Peter 5:8.) You have an adversary who hates you. He is working day and night to try to destroy your life, home, health, finances and all that you have. As believers, we have total authority over Satan and his kingdom. However, many Christians have abdicated their authority by being ignorant of it.

THE JESUS GENERATION

As the leader of God's people, Joshua is a beautiful type of Jesus Christ, the Lord of the Church. Joshua means "the Lord's salvation; the Savior." It is the Hebrew equivalent to the name Jesus. We are the Joshua Generation -- the Jesus Generation!

Joshua did something in Joshua 10:24-26 that is a picture of what Christ did for us at Calvary: "So it was, when they brought out those kings to Joshua, that Joshua called for all the men of Israel, and said to the captains of the men of war who went with him, 'Come near, put your feet on the necks of these kings.' And they drew near and put their feet on their necks. Then Joshua said to them, 'Do not be afraid, nor be dismayed; be strong and of good courage, for thus the LORD will do to all your enemies against whom you fight.' And afterward Joshua struck them and killed them, and hanged them on five trees; and they were hanging on the trees until evening."

In verse 24, we see that Joshua told the leaders of Israel to put their feet on the necks of these kings. These five kings are a type of Satan's government in the earth. Jesus has given us authority to literally stomp on the neck of Satan's authority! "Far above all principality and power and might and dominion, and every name that is named, not only in this age but also in that which is to come. And He put all things under His feet, and gave Him to be head over all things to the church, which is His body, the fullness of Him who fills all in all." (Ephesians 1:21-22.) All things are under Christ! As the Body of Christ in the earth, all things are under our feet!

In verse 26, Joshua smote and killed these five kings and hung them on five trees. What a powerful picture of the victory that Christ obtained for us on the Cross (tree) of Calvary! Not only did the Cross free us from the power of sin and death, it also freed us from the one who used that power over us -- Satan.

Take a look at this powerful verse: "Having disarmed principalities and powers, He made a public spectacle of them, triumphing over them in it." (Colossians 2:15.) The NIV translation of this verse reads: "And having disarmed the powers and authorities, he made a public spectacle of them, triumphing over them by the cross."

The Cross is our place of forgiveness, redemption and total victory. Two thousand years ago, the sins of this world were remitted and forgiven at Calvary. No one will ever go to hell because of their "sins." The only way to go to hell is to not accept or believe that Christ bore your sins at Calvary. This is the grace of God for us. The five trees (or "crosses") mentioned in Joshua 10:26 are a picture of God's grace. Five is the number of God's grace. Part of the provision of God's grace for us is that, at Calvary, God made us "more than conquerors" over Satan's kingdom. "You are of God, little children, and have overcome them, because He who is in you is greater than he who is in the world." (1 John 4:4.)

When we are born again, we are brought into the Kingdom of God, and in His Kingdom, we've been given authority over all the works of the enemy. In your life, family, city and nation, you've been given power and authority over all the strength of the enemy. It is time for us to retake our families and cities for God. Jesus told us we would "tread upon serpents and scorpions."

The serpents and scorpions that Jesus speaks of here are not the snakes and insects of the natural desert, but they are types and levels of Satan's kingdom. Jesus told us to "put our feet on the necks" of the kingdom of Satan. We must put on our "boots" of authority, and in the name of Jesus crush the evil spirits that want to control our lives and families and cities.

How sad it is that the church, the Body of Christ, has watched helplessly and hopelessly as Satan has ripped off our lives and families and cities! Many poor, deceived saints have said "it was just God's will" when Satan came to destroy, steal and kill in their lives and circumstances. It is Satan who comes to destroy and steal from us. "The thief does not come except to steal, and to kill, and to destroy. I have come that they may have life, and that they may have it more abundantly." (John 10:10.)

In this verse, Jesus gives us Satan's job description. Satan
has come to steal, kill and destroy. Jesus has come to bring
abundant life! We must wake up and spiritually discern what
is of God and what is of Satan. If you take Satan out of the
picture like Job did, then you must hold God responsible for
both good and bad. However, there is absolutely no bad in
God! "Every good gift and every perfect gift is from above,
and comes down from the Father of lights, with whom there
is no variation or shadow of turning." (James 1:17.)

As we begin to understand our authority as believers, and
as we begin to operate in that authority, the Kingdom of God
is strengthened, and Satan's kingdom is weakened. Satan rules
now by deception, and is illegally operating his kingdom. As
you begin to speak and exercise your authority as a son or
daughter of God, your life and family will be loosed from the
unseen control of Satan's army.

As believers accept and exercise their authority in a city, the
dark, evil, destructive powers that control the unsaved and
spiritually ignorant souls of that city begin to lose their power
and influence over the minds and hearts of those people. As
God's people discern and destroy the ruling spirits in their
geographical area, the city and area will experience an "open
heaven." This condition of an "open heaven" allows the Word
of God to produce life, and revival will be the result.

In Luke 10:17, 18, Jesus describes this weakening of Satan's kingdom when we exercise our rights and authority: "Then the seventy returned with joy, saying, 'Lord, even the demons are subject to us in Your name.' And He said to them, 'I saw Satan fall like lightning from heaven.'"

After the disciples came back rejoicing in their new-found authority over demons, Jesus said He "beheld Satan as lightning fall from heaven." Jesus was describing the weakening of Satan's kingdom by Jesus' disciples exercising their authority over devils. As God's people understand and practice their God-given authority over Satan's army, the Kingdom of God is advanced, and Satan's kingdom is pushed back.

EXERCISING OUR AUTHORITY

Many ministers and denominations today completely ignore the devil, and they ridicule and belittle those who preach spiritual warfare and the authority of the believer. However, if Jesus and His disciples considered teaching on spiritual warfare and the authority of the believer vitally important, then I think we're in good company in teaching God's people to discern and destroy Satan's influence and dominion over their lives, families and cities.

Jesus taught about the importance and responsibility of exercising authority over our enemy. "'If Satan also is divided against himself, how will his kingdom stand? Because you say

I cast out demons by Beelzebub. And if I cast out demons by Beelzebub, by whom do your sons cast them out? Therefore they will be your judges. But if I cast out demons with the finger of God, surely the kingdom of God has come upon you. When a strong man, fully armed, guards his own palace, his goods are in peace. But when a stronger than he comes upon him and overcomes him, he takes from him all his armor in which he trusted, and divides his spoils.'" (Luke 11:18-22.)

The "strong man" is that demonic power that has control over people, families, cities and nations. This strong man must be conquered before his "goods" can be spoiled. As we bind the strong man through prayer in the name of Jesus, we then can see God's Kingdom come to our lives, families, cities and nations.

Jesus said that the binding of the strong man was the first step to taking his goods. We read in Matthew 16:19: "'And I will give you the keys of the kingdom of heaven, and whatever you bind on earth will be bound in heaven, and whatever you loose on earth will be loosed in heaven.'"

The preaching of the Gospel and the work of the ministry must be preceded by prayer (spiritual warfare) that addresses the strong man being dealt with. Without bathing our works in intercession, we doom our efforts to mediocre results at best.

EXPOSING THE EVIL SPIRITUAL RULERS

We live in the hour of Satan's greatest attack against mankind. But we also live in the greatest hour of the church. These two kingdoms are in a titanic struggle for the souls of this generation. God, by His Spirit, has begun to reveal to individuals and leaders the "strong man" over families and cities and nations.

It is God's will to expose these evil spiritual rulers in order for His people to rise up in power and authority to bind and defeat them. 1 John 4:1 tells us to "not believe every spirit , but test the spirits, whether they are of God; because many false prophets have gone out into the world." We are to "test" (discern, examine, prove, test) the spirits at work in our world. Ignorance is Satan's greatest weapon against the church! We are not to be ignorant of Satan's strategies and strongholds "lest Satan should take advantage of us; for we are not ignorant of his devices." (2 Corinthians 2:11.)

This scripture tells us that ignorance gives Satan the advantage over us. Through the Holy Spirit, we are to discern and destory the work of Satan. This spiritual discovery gives us the advantage over him! To the equipped and empowered believer, victory begins the very moment that Satan's influence is discovered. God reveals spiritual things in order for us to pray and act accordingly.

GOD'S HEARTBEAT

In Psalm 2:8-10, we see God's heartbeat for us to believe Him for our cities and nations: "'Ask of Me, and I will give You the nations for Your inheritance, and the ends of the earth for Your possession. You shall break them with a rod of iron; you shall dash them to pieces like a potter's vessel.' Now therefore, be wise, O kings; be instructed, you judges of the earth."

As we intercede for our families, cities and nations, God gives us a possessing spirit. We begin to know with a great confidence that it is God's will to save and deliver those we pray for. Then God give us the strength and authority to "dash in pieces" the strongholds over their lives.

We are to "be wise" and "be instructed" in the realm of spiritual warfare. When Satan's stronghold is pulled down, then the Gospel has a free course and will always prosper and produce. A lack of discerning and diligent spiritual warfare is, in effect, surrender by default to the strong man of the enemy.

When you study the life of the kings of the nation of Israel, you see that God always makes mention of how they treated the "high places" during their reign. These high places were groves, temples and altars where false gods were worshipped and pagan religions were practiced. Although many of these kings did right in the sight of God (like many ministers today have and are doing right in God's eyes), by not addressing the "false gods" and "high places", they did not fight for the people of God. It is not enough for us to be content and satisfied with our own salvation and our nice little churches. We must contend with the "high places" of demonic power over those all around us! God is ready to give us the "treasures" of cities and nations as we follow Him fully and pull down and destroy Satan's domain.

Isaiah 45:2-3 reads: "I will go before you and make the crooked places straight; I will break in pieces the gates of bronze and cut the bars of iron. I will give you the treasures of darkness and hidden riches of secret places, that you may know that I, the LORD, who call you by your name, am the God of Israel."

The "gates" over our families and cities can be broken by the prayer of God's people. As we respond to God's invitation to pray for our families and cities, God delights in giving us the "treasures of darkness" and the "hidden riches of secret places."

It is our responsibility -- our obligation as the children of God -- to realize and respond to the Heartbeat of God. That heartbeat is for a lost, wounded, imprisoned world to come to Him. How can those in prison free themselves? They can't! Then how is the person who is unsaved and enslaved to Satan freed? By the intercession of God's people!

Isaiah 66:8 asks, "Who has heard such a thing? Who has

THE JOSHUA GENERATION // 175

seen such things? Shall the earth be made to give birth in one day? Or shall a nation be born at once? For as soon as Zion was in labor, She gave birth to her children." As soon as the Church (Hebrews 12:22 tells us Zion is a type of the Church) begins to intercede (Galatians 4:19 tells us travailing is a picture of intercession), new life occurs. Children are born!

Paul, in 1 Timothy 2:1-4, says, "Therefore I exhort first of all that supplications, prayers, intercessions, and giving of thanks be made for all men, for kings and all who are in authority, that we may lead a quiet and peaceable life in all godliness and reverence. For this is good and acceptable in the sight of God our Savior, who desires all men to be saved and to come to the knowledge of the truth."

As we pray for "all men" that they would "be saved and come unto the knowledge of the truth," the Spirit of God will bring in a harvest of men's souls into the Kingdom of God.

TIME TO WAKE UP

God is giving us a wake-up call in this hour.

The Joshua Generation is that company of believers who have heard the trumpet of the Spirit calling the church to warfare.

"Proclaim this among the nations: 'Prepare for war! Wake up the mighty men, let all the men of war draw near, let them come up. Beat your plowshares into swords and your pruning hooks into spears; let the weak say, "I am strong." Assemble and come, all you nations, and gather together all around. Cause your mighty ones to go down there, O LORD.'" (Joel 3:9-11.)

There is no one mightier in the earth than the Church of Jesus Christ. It is time for us to wake up! We are to put on God's strength and power. We are to cause the mighty ones to come down. We are to dethrone the principalities and powers that hold our cities in bondage.

The greatest harvest of souls the church has ever seen is, even now, beginning to be reaped. As we see Joel prophesied: "Put in the sickle, for the harvest is ripe. Come, go down; for the winepress is full, the vats overflow -- for their wickedness is great. Multitudes, multitudes in the valley of decision! For the day of the LORD is near in the valley of decision." (Joel 3:13, 14.)

This ingathering of untold millions, and eventually billions, is the result of God's people entering into spiritual warfare by understanding and practicing their spiritual authority over the kingdom of Satan. Let us "run to the battle" and see our families, cities and nations brought into the Kingdom and life of our God!

Joshua 10:25-26 tells us to "not be afraid, nor be dismayed; be strong and of good courage, for thus the LORD will do to all your enemies against whom you fight."

CHAPTER 20:
LOOKING FOR TROUBLE

Joshua 7:1 tells us that "the Israelites acted unfaithfully in regard to the devoted things; Achan son of Carmi, the son of Zimri, the son of Zerah, of the tribe of Judah, took some of them. So the LORD's anger burned against Israel." (NIV)

Achan's name means "troubler," and his sin literally stopped the children of Israel from conquering the city of Ai. God had spoken to Joshua that all of the gold and silver and valuable possessions of the city of Jericho should be brought into the treasury of Israel for the building of the Temple. We read about this in Joshua 6:18-19: "'But keep away from the devoted things, so that you will not bring about your own destruction by taking any of them. Otherwise you will make the camp of Israel liable to destruction and bring trouble on it. All the silver and gold and the articles of bronze and iron are sacred to the LORD and must go into his treasury.'"

(NIV)

Also, in Joshua 6:24: "Then they burned the whole city and everything in it, but they put the silver and gold and the articles of bronze and iron into the treasury of the LORD's house." (NIV)

The Lord called the gold and silver and valuable possessions "devoted things." This speaks of two types of devotion. First of all, these valuable things were used by pagan, ungodly people in various fleshly and demonic, sinful practices. But more importantly, these valuable items were wanted by God. He wanted the first fruits of Canaan dedicated to Him. For the sake of building the Temple, these valued possessions had been "devoted" to God's purposes by God Himself.

In a congregation of several million people, there were a lot of people "sinning." They faced the same temptations and battles that we face. However, this one sin by Achan stopped an entire nation and brought about the anger of God. This sin deals with the love of money. Achan coveted after those valuable possessions, and the spirit of greed filled his heart.

We see this exact sin duplicated in the Early Church. "But a certain man named Ananias, with Sapphira his wife, sold a possession. And he kept back part of the proceeds, his wife also being aware of it, and brought a certain part and laid it at the apostles' feet. But Peter said, 'Ananias, why has Satan filled your heart to lie to the Holy Spirit and keep back part of the price of the land for yourself? While it remained, was it not your own? And after it was sold, was it not in your own control? Why have you conceived this thing in your heart? You have not lied to men but to God.'

"Then Ananias, hearing these words, fell down and breathed his last. So great fear came upon all those who heard these things. And the young men arose and wrapped him up, carried him out, and buried him.

"Now it was about three hours later when his wife came in, not knowing what had happened. And Peter answered her, 'Tell me whether you sold the land for so much?' She said, 'Yes, for so much.' Then Peter said to her, 'How is it that you have agreed together to test the Spirit of the Lord? Look, the feet of those who have buried your husband are at the door, and they will carry you out.'

"Then immediately she fell down at his feet and breathed her last. And the young men came in and found her dead, and carrying her out, buried her by her husband.11 So great fear came upon all the church and upon all who heard these things." (Acts 5:1-11.)

This is the first recorded sin in the Early Church, and it was Satan's first great attack against the Church ("How is it that Satan has filled your heart?"). Both in this example and in the example of Achan's sin, we see that our response to money is crucial to God. In both of these instances, the two men lied and deceived because of greed.

The Joshua Generation must respond rightly to God in giving and attitudes about finances.

We read in 1 Timothy 6:9, 10 (NIV): "People who want to get rich fall into temptation and a trap and into many foolish and harmful desires that plunge men into ruin and destruction. For the love of money is a root of all kinds of evil. Some people, eager for money, have wandered from the faith and pierced themselves with many griefs." The sin of the love of money is one of Satan's greatest weapons and temptations for all of man.

You may think that God doesn't notice the way you give and the way you handle finances, but He does! In fact, the way you respond to God financially reveals what is truly in your heart. The Early Church was so completely dedicated to God's will and the furtherance of His Kingdom that they abandoned all personal rights to possessions and finances. They literally laid their money and possessions at the Apostles' feet.

The spirit of sacrificial giving is one of the keys for revival found in the book of Acts. "Now all who believed were together, and had all things in common, and sold their possessions and goods, and divided them among all, as anyone had need." (Acts 2:44, 45.) "Nor was there anyone among them who lacked; for all who were possessors of lands or houses sold them, and brought the proceeds of the things that were sold, and laid them at the apostles' feet; and they distributed to each as anyone had need." (Acts 4:34, 35.)

For many years, ministers have sheepishly and timidly received offerings and spoken of finances in the church. That is going to stop! Ministers must boldly teach God's Word to God's people in order to free them from the curse of covetousness and poverty and greed.

If you do not faithfully and consistently tithe and give offerings, then you are a God-robber and have "troubled" your life, family and church! "'Will a man rob God? Yet you have robbed Me! But you say, "In what way have we robbed You?" In tithes and offerings. You are cursed with a curse, for you have robbed Me, even this whole nation. Bring all the tithes into the storehouse, that there may be food in My house, and try Me now in this,' says the LORD of hosts, 'If I will not open for you the windows of heaven and pour out for you such blessing that there will not be room enough to receive it. And I will rebuke the devourer for your sakes, so that he will not destroy the fruit of your ground, nor shall the vine fail to bear fruit for you in the field,' says the LORD of hosts; 'and all nations will call you blessed, for you will be a delightful land,' says the LORD of hosts." (Malachi 3:8-12.)

No matter why you say you don't tithe and give, the real reason is the love of money in your life.

Yes, even Spirit-filled believers who say they love God are "cursed with a curse" if they have not tithed and given offerings. It is very simple, dear saint, God will not be mocked. If you have robbed God, then ask him for forgiveness and begin to tithe and give offerings immediately!

Just as the Holy Spirit exposed this sin of the love of money in the Book of Acts, God gave Joshua a "word of knowledge" that it was Achan who troubled Israel with his sin. (You are bringing "spiritual trouble" to your family and church if you don't tithe and give. Your sin affects more than just you.)

Joshua 7:19-21 tells us: "Now Joshua said to Achan, 'My son, I beg you, give glory to the LORD God of Israel, and make confession to Him, and tell me now what you have done; do not hide it from me.' And Achan answered Joshua and said, 'Indeed I have sinned against the LORD God of Israel, and this is what I have done: When I saw among the spoils a beautiful Babylonian garment, two hundred shekels of silver, and a wedge of gold weighing fifty shekels, I coveted them and took them. And there they are, hidden in the earth in the midst of my tent, with the silver under it.'"

In these coming days, God will expose and judge those who have dealt deceitfully with His Church in its finances.

Joshua was praying a defeated and discouraged prayer to God asking why the army had be defeated by the men of the city of Ai. As he was "whining" to God, God interrupted and rebuked him and told him to consecrate the people. We are going to be consecrated and made holy in these last days by strong, anointed preaching and teaching that will confront sin in our lives.

When Achan was caught, he was stoned and burned. "And Joshua said, 'Why have you troubled us? The LORD will trouble you this day.' So all Israel stoned him with stones; and they burned them with fire after they had stoned them with stones. Then they raised over him a great heap of stones, still there to this day. So the LORD turned from the fierceness of His anger. Therefore the name of that place has been called the Valley of Achor to this day." (Joshua 7:25, 26.)

By the fire of God's Holy Spirit, and by the power of His Word, we can destroy the spirit of Achan from our lives. As we surrender our entire lives to God, we will be willing to freely and joyfully give all we possess to God. As we build God's Kingdom, His Kingdom builds us.

God is not against you having things; He is against things having you! "Do not be deceived, God is not mocked; for whatever a man sows, that he will also reap. For he who sows to his flesh will of the flesh reap corruption, but he who sows to the Spirit will of the Spirit reap everlasting life. And let us not grow weary while doing good, for in due season we shall reap if we do not lose heart. Therefore, as we have opportunity, let us do good to all, especially to those who are of the household of faith." (Galatians 6:7-10.)

God will not be mocked. We cannot continue to come to church and receive from God if we are robbing Him. In many churches, there are more "non-tithers" than tithers! How can God move there? He is limited because they (the "non-tithers") have troubled their church.

God wants to meet your needs and make you a blessing to His people, but He can only respond to the way we give. "But this I say: He who sows sparingly will also reap sparingly, and he who sows bountifully will also reap bountifully. So let each one give as he purposes in his heart, not grudgingly or of necessity; for God loves a cheerful giver. And God is able to make all grace abound toward you, that you, always having all sufficiency in all things, may have an abundance for every good work." (2 Corinthians 9:6-8.)

There is no greater joy in life than to give. There is no greater fulfillment in life than to develop a lifestyle of giving. Why? Because God has "freely given" and He expects us to "freely give." Learn to be a giver and then you will live to give and become a channel of God's blessings to those around you.

CHAPTER 21: CITIES OF REFUGE

The Lord instructed Joshua to build six unique cities to be called cities of refuge. These six cities were all built high on hillsides and could be seen for miles around. They were dispersed throughout the Promised Land so they could be reached from any place. The purpose of these six cities of refuge was to be a shelter of protection for those who had innocently shed blood (accidental deaths).

We read in Joshua 20:1-6: "The LORD also spoke to Joshua, saying, 'Speak to the children of Israel, saying: "Appoint for yourselves cities of refuge, of which I spoke to you through Moses, that the slayer who kills a person accidentally or unintentionally may flee there; and they shall be your refuge from the avenger of blood. And when he flees to one of those cities, and stands at the entrance of the gate of the city, and declares his case in the hearing of the elders of that city, they shall take him into the city as one of them, and give him a place, that he may dwell among them. Then if the avenger of blood pursues him, they shall not deliver the slayer into his hand, because he struck his neighbor unintentionally, but did not hate him beforehand. And he shall dwell in that city until he stands before the congregation for judgment, and until the death of the one who is high priest in those days. Then the slayer may return and come to his own city and his own house, to the city from which he fled.'"

The city of refuge is a type of the last day church in the earth! By the Blood of Jesus we have been delivered from our "sin" nature, and also from the enemy (avenger) of our soul. The church is to be a "city on a hill" just like the city of refuge was. We are to be a visible demonstration of God's Kingdom to the world. Jesus said, "You are the light of the world. A city that is set on a hill cannot be hidden." (Matthew 5:14.)

The Body – the ministry and life of a local church -- is to be God's place of refuge for our desperate world. The church is a place of protection, power and peace for all those who enter into God's Kingdom. These six different cities received six different callings and anointings that last day Church will have.

SIX CITIES OF REFUGE

God desires to raise every city of the world up as a

refuge. The Book of Joshua and the Book of Ephesians gives us greater understanding of cities that God ordained to be places of refuge. These six beautiful cities are pictures that reveal the ministry of the last day Church.

1. Kadesh: "Holy Sanctuary"

The first city of refuge was Kadesh means "holy sanctuary." (Joshua 20:7.) The church is to be the holy sanctuary or temple of God's presence. As born-again believers, we become the temple of God's very presence. Ephesians 2:21-22 says, "in whom the whole building, being fitted together, grows into a holy temple in the Lord, in whom you also are being built together for a dwelling place of God in the Spirit." As we come together as the corporate temple of the Lord, God's presence is multiplied and magnified in the earth.

God has always desired to dwell with and in man. We are His temple that He dwells in by the Holy Spirit. "Do you not know that you are the temple of God and that the Spirit of God dwells in you?" (1 Corinthians 3:16.) "Or do you not know that your body is the temple of the Holy Spirit who is in you, whom you have from God, and you are not your own?" (1 Corinthians 6:19.) "And what agreement has the temple of God with idols? For you are the temple of the living God. As God has said: 'I will dwell in them and walk among them. I will be their God, and they shall be My people.'" (2 Corinthians 6:16.)

The presence of God is becoming stronger and stronger in the church. God is going to let His full presence be seen in the church. When God's presence and glory are in our midst, revival is the natural result.

2. Shechem: "The Shoulder"

The second city of refuge that God told Joshua to establish was Shechem which means "the shoulder" and is a type of the government of God. "For unto us a Child is born, unto us a Son is given; and the government will be upon His shoulder. And His name will be called Wonderful, Counselor, Mighty God, Everlasting Father, Prince of Peace." (Isaiah 9:6)

"The government shall be upon his shoulder." This is a picture of the restoration of the five-fold ministry in the church.

The last day Joshua Generation Church will be a place where God's government is in control!

In much of the church there is a "head problem" -- a problem caused because the church's government does not follow God's pattern and order. We must follow the plan of God given to us in the Word of God for our church government. In Ephesians, we see that the government of God is for the Body of Christ. "And He Himself gave some to be apostles, some prophets, some evangelists, and some pastors and teachers, for the equipping of the saints for the work of ministry, for the edifying of the Body of Christ, till we all come to the unity of the faith and of the knowledge of the Son of God, to a perfect man, to the measure of the stature of the fullness of Christ; that we should no longer be children, tossed to and fro and carried about with every wind of doctrine, by the trickery of men, in the cunning craftiness of deceitful plotting, but, speaking the truth in love, may grow up in all things into Him who is the head -- Christ -- from whom the whole body, joined and knit together by what every joint supplies, according to the effective working by which every part does its share, causes growth of the body for the edifying of itself in love." (Ephesians 4:11-16.)

Shechem is a type of the Body of Christ in the earth, and the body can only function in relationship and harmony to its head. God's government brings a "divine order" and safety into the Church. God is restoring the office and ministry of the Apostle and Prophet. As He does, there is coming a new maturity and order to the Body of Christ.

In the last-day church, we will see these five ministry offices flowing together in team ministry. As each minister finds his place in God's order, and receives and releases the other four offices, the Body of Christ will experience tremendous growth and maturity. God's pattern will produce God's power in the Church.

3. Hebron: "Communion, Fellowship"

The third city of refuge that God instructed Joshua to establish was Kirjath Arba or Hebron. It means "communion, fellowship." (Joshua 20:7.) The Joshua Generation Church is a place of communion and fellowship with God, and also with one another. This place is pictured in Ephesians in the marriage relationship between husband and wife. "For the husband is head of the wife, as also Christ is head of the church; and He is the Savior of the body. Therefore, just as the church is subject to Christ, so let the wives be to their own husbands in everything.

"Husbands, love your wives, just as Christ also loved the church and gave Himself for her, that He might sanctify and cleanse her with the washing of water by the word, that He might present her to Himself a glorious church, not having spot or wrinkle or any such thing, but that she should be holy and without blemish. So husbands ought to love their own wives as their own bodies; he who loves his wife loves himself. For no one ever hated his own flesh, but nourishes and cherishes it, just as the Lord does the church. For we are members of His body, of His flesh and of His bones. 'For this reason a man shall leave his father and mother and be joined to his wife, and the two shall become one flesh.' This is a great mystery, but I speak concerning Christ and the church." (Ephesians 5:23-32.)

We are the Bride of Christ in the earth. We love, relate and respond to our Lord in the same way a Bride lovingly responds to her husband. Our loving God longs for relationship and fellowship with His "Bride" in the earth.

In this beautiful picture of the Bride and Bridegroom, we find several powerful principles that not only flow between our Lord and us, but are also meant to flow in our interpersonal relationships in the church.

The first principle we see in Ephesians is that the church is to be in submission to the Lord, as a wife is to be to her husband. Submission releases the Lord to be our Savior. Submission also releases the Lord to be our Deliverer. The Lord responds with His protecting, delivering power to the submitted believer.

Husbands are to love their wives as Christ loves the Church and "gave himself for it." Love is to flow from Christ into us, and then into one another. The glorious church is a church filled with the love of God for one another and for the world. The Bride of Christ will radiate God's glory as we receive and release God's love.

The Church is washed clean by the water of the Word of Christ. It is God's Word that purifies and sanctifies the church. We also see the power of our words spoken to one another to "wash" each other with God's Word.

As the Church becomes committed and submitted to God and to each other, we will see the power of God's love flow from us to our hurting world.

Everything that God does in ministry, He does through the law of relationship. Our relationship with Christ is to produce fruit. Our relationship to one another is also to produce fruit. The church is to be a place of thriving relationships that produce healed and restored lives. God wants to heal you and restore your life, and He will do it through your relationship with Him and with His people.

4. Bezer: "Fortress, Stronghold"

The fourth city of refuge that God told Joshua to establish was Bezer. Bezer means "fortress, stronghold" and is a picture of the army of God in the earth. In every city of the world, God wants to establish a stronghold or a fortification of His might and power.

Ephesians 6:10-18 tells us: "Finally, my brethren, be strong in the Lord and in the power of His might. Put on the whole armor of God, that you may be able to stand against the Wiles of the devil. For we do not wrestle against flesh and blood, but against principalities, against powers, against the rulers of the darkness of this age, against spiritual hosts of wickedness in the heavenly places. Therefore take up the whole armor of God, that you may be able to withstand in the evil day, and having done all, to stand.

"Stand therefore, having girded your waist with truth, having put on the breastplate of righteousness, and having shod your feet with the preparation of the Gospel of peace; above all, taking the shield of faith with which you will be able to quench all the fiery Darts of the wicked one. And take the helmet of salvation, and the sword of the Spirit, which is the word of God; praying always with all prayer and supplication in the Spirit, being watchful to this end with all perseverance and supplication for all the saints."

We see here that the church is to be "dressed for war" by putting on the armor of God. We're commanded to "be strong in the Lord." The end-time church will be a warring church, not warring against flesh and blood, but against our enemy and his kingdom. "For though we walk in the flesh, we do not war according to the flesh. For the weapons of our warfare are not carnal but mighty in God for pulling down strongholds, casting down arguments and every high thing that exalts itself against the knowledge of God, bringing every thought into captivity to the obedience of Christ." (2 Corinthians 10:3-5.)

Much of the language in the New Testament is military in tone. It was written as a training manual for the army of God in the earth. Writing to Timothy, Paul states, "You therefore must endure hardship as a good soldier of Jesus Christ. No one engaged in warfare entangles himself with the affairs of this life, that he may please him who enlisted him as a soldier." (2 Timothy 2:3, 4.)

The Lord instructed Moses that, at the appointed time of battle, when they would fight the enemies of God, to let all the warring men of Israel shout with one accord, "Let God arise and His enemies be scattered!" Let us, as the army of God in the earth, join together and shout, "Let God arise and His enemies be scattered!"

5. Ramoth: "High, Exalted Place"

The fifth city of refuge was called Ramoth. Ramoth means "high, exalted place" and is a picture of our exalted place in Christ. Ephesians 2:6-7 tells us that God "raised us up together, and made us sit together in the heavenly places in Christ Jesus, that in the ages to come He might show the exceeding riches of His grace in His kindness toward us in Christ Jesus."

We are seated in "heavenly places" through Jesus Christ. We have freely been given a place of honor and exaltation right next to Jesus Christ in heaven! Not only that, but we have been given all that heaven has through Jesus.

This not only speaks of our ruling and reigning with Christ after He comes back for us, but it also speaks of our position and inheritance in this life. The Word of God is our legal inheritance from God. To know and believe the precious promises of God's Word is to live in our exalted place in Christ. God's Word is filled with literally thousands of precious promises that God has given us as our inheritance in Him. All these promises are for us. We read about this in 2 Corinthians 1:20: "For all the promises of God in Him are Yes, and in Him Amen, to the glory of God through us."

God longs for us to know and believe in what He has done for us. "That the God of our Lord Jesus Christ, the Father of glory, may give to you the spirit of wisdom and revelation in the knowledge of Him, the eyes of your understanding being enlightened; that you may know what is the hope of His calling, what are the riches of the glory of His inheritance in the saints, and what is the exceeding greatness of His power toward us who believe, according to the working of His mighty power." (Ephesians 1:17-19.)

The Holy Spirit will show us:

Who we are in Christ
What we have in Christ
What we can do through Christ

We are literally "more than conquerors" right now in Jesus Christ. When you believe that and then live it, you will begin to experience the life and power God has made available to you.

6. Bashan: "Fruitfulness, Fertile Soil"

The sixth city of refuge was in Bashan. Bashan means "fruitfulness, fertile soil." The church is to be a place where we produce the fruit and evidence of God's Word. God's Word will always change lives when it is received properly.

This place of fruitfulness is spoken of in Ephesians as being the children of God. God "predestined us to adoption as sons by Jesus Christ to Himself, according to the good pleasure of His will." (Ephesians 1:5.) "Now, therefore, you are no longer strangers and foreigners, but fellow citizens with the saints and members of the household of God." (Ephesians 2:19.) We are the children of God in the earth. As the children of a loving Father, we've been given a glorious inheritance revealed to us in God's Word.

According to Ephesians 1:11: "In Him also we have

obtained an inheritance, being predestined according to
the purpose of Him who works all things according to the
counsel of His will." And in Ephesians 1:18-19, God wants
us to "know what is the hope of His calling, what are the
riches of the glory of His inheritance in the saints."

As the children of God, our lives are "fertile soil" for our
Father's Word to produce life. We desire to emulate and
imitate our Heavenly Father just as natural children do.
"Therefore be imitators of God as dear children. And walk
in love, as Christ also has loved us and given Himself for
us, an offering and a sacrifice to God for a sweet-smelling
aroma." (Ephesians 5:1, 2.) When we "walk in love," we
produce the fruit of the Spirit and reveal God's nature in
us. Fruitfulness, for the believer, begins by knowing and
believing God's great love for you and sharing that love
with others.

God's purpose is for the world to see His love in us.
By walking in this love, we clothe ourselves in love. Dear
believer, God is love, and when you begin to know and
experience His love for you, your whole life will change.
Why? Because loved people love people! The basis for all
Christian victory and success is in the knowing and the
experiencing of God's love.

We read in Ephesians 3:16-20 that Paul prayed God
would "grant you, according to the riches of His glory, to

be strengthened with might through His Spirit in the inner man, that Christ may dwell in your hearts through faith; that you, being rooted and grounded in love, may be able to comprehend with all the saints what is the width and length and depth and height -- to know the love of Christ which passes knowledge; that you may be filled with all the fullness of God. Now to Him who is able to do exceedingly abundantly above all that we ask or think, according to the power that works in us."

We can be filled with the "fullness of God" by believing in and receiving the love of God. After we know and believe in this love, we are able to love each other. This love is a light to a dark world. "For you were once darkness, but now you are light in the Lord. Walk as children of light." (Ephesians 5:8.) Let us walk in love (and thus walk in the light) and release God's glory and life to our hurting world.

The Joshua Generation Church is a place of refuge for a hurting world.

The church must not be hidden and isolated, but instead be "on a hill" to be seen of all men. We have what the world needs: JESUS! His life, Spirit and Word will save, heal and deliver any and all that receive Him.

Does your city know about you and your church? Are we

seeking God's supernatural solutions to the needs and problems of our cities? In these last days, God wants to establish "churches (cities) of refuge" in every city of the world. He wants to establish a place where His life and love flow out to the needs of humanity, a place where solutions and answers and miracles are given to searching lives.

Let us pray and work to build the Kingdom of God where we live for in the rule and reign of Christ shall the needs and answers of a dying world be met.

ABOUT THE AUTHOR

Dr. Michael Maiden is the founder and senior pastor of Church For The Nations, a prophetic church located in Phoenix, Arizona. Dr. Maiden is a strong prophetic voice to this generation. His teachings are timely, relevant and life changing. He has been pastoring in the valley of the sun for over 20 years.

Dr. Maiden serves as the Southwest Director for Church on the Rock International, a dynamic network of ministers, pastors, evangelists and missionaries who are joining hearts and hands in reaching the world for Jesus.

Dr. Maiden and his wife, Mary, live in Phoenix, Arizona with their four children.

JOSHUA GENERATION PUBLSHING

For more information about this book and other resources from Dr. Michael Maiden please contact Joshua Generation Publishing at:

Joshua Generation Publishing
11640 N 19th Ave
Phoenix AZ 85029

or call

602.861.0000